77 Ways

TO PRAY WITH
YOUR KIDS

JERRY WINDLEY-DAOUST

BEACON

Nihil Obstat: Rev. Timothy Hall
                Censor Librorum
                24 December 2014

Imprimatur: † Most Rev. John Quinn
                Bishop of Winona
                24 December 2014

The imprimatur is an official declaration that a book or pamphlet is free
of doctrinal or moral error. No implication is contained therein that those
who have granted the imprimatur agree with the contents, opinions, or
statements expressed.

Scripture quotations are from New Revised Standard Version Bible: Catholic
Edition, copyright © 1989, 1993 National Council of the Churches of Christ in
the United States of America. Used by permission. All rights reserved.

Quotes are taken from the English translation of the *Catechism of the
Catholic Church* for the United States of America (indicated as *CCC*), 2nd
ed. Copyright 1997 by United States Catholic Conference—Libreria Editrice
Vaticana.

The "Examination of Conscience for Children" is by Fr. Thomas Weinandy,
and may be reproduced and distributed free of charge by permission of the
author.

Printed in the United States of America [1]

LIBRARY OF CONGRESS CATALOGING-IN-PUBLICATION DATA
Windley-Daoust, Jerry, author.
77 ways to pray with your kids : a guide for Catholic families / Jerry
Windley-Daoust.
Other titles: Seventy-seven ways to pray with your kids
Description: North Palm Beach : Beacon Publishing, 2016. | Originally
published: Winona, MN : Gracewatch Media, 2014. | Includes index.
LCCN 2016028220| ISBN 9781942611790 (hardcover) | ISBN
9781942611806 (softcover) | ISBN 9781942611813 (ebook)
LCSH: Prayer--Catholic Church. | Families--Religious life.
210.3 .W555 2016
249—dc23

                                            2016028220

TABLE *of* CONTENTS

Q & A :

How to Use This Book

I don't know how to pray, much less how to pray with my kids. Is this book for me?

If you would like to improve your family prayer life, then this book is for you, no matter what your current prayer life looks like. Here are some of the key features of *77 Ways to Pray with Your Kids*:

Many ways of praying. This book is a comprehensive collection of the many ways Catholics pray, including both traditional and more modern practices. If you are just beginning to pray together as a family, you can explore these possibilities to find the best way to begin. If your family already prays together, you can enrich your family prayer time by trying out some new prayer practices.

Get going quickly. The short, stand-alone articles in this book will get you going on a family prayer activity quickly, usually with less than five minutes of reading time. Activities tagged "Easy" require no advance preparation.

Ideas for young children, older kids, and teens. Each way of praying is tagged to indicate its appropriateness for younger children (ages three to six), older kids (ages seven to twelve), and teens (ages thirteen to eighteen). Articles about practices that work with kids of any age (for example, the rosary) may offer strategies for modifying the practice to be more appropriate for different age groups.

Talking points. Sometimes your kids may have questions about a particular prayer practice: "Why do we pray with images?" "Why do we pray for the dead?" "Why do we go to confession?" Many of the articles in this book include a ***Talking Points*** section that offers a brief explanation of a particular prayer practice; you can use this information as a starting point for discussion.

Ways to learn more. If you need to go deeper, you can refer to the sources listed under the "Learn more" heading. These sources include the *Catechism of the Catholic Church*, Scriptures, or other Church documents that provide more information about a prayer practice. You can find these documents online by searching under their title (or the Scripture citation, or the word *catechism* plus the paragraph number).

Why should I teach my children to pray?

Prayer is a living relationship with God, who is our source, our destiny, and our way to happiness in this life and the next. If you want your kids to have a rich, life-giving friendship with God, then it will be well worth the extra time and effort to teach them how to enter into God's presence through prayer.

"The evidence clearly shows that the single most important social influence on the religious and spiritual lives of adolescents is their parents," according to the National Study on Youth and Religion, a research project directed by Christian Smith, professor of sociology at the University of Notre Dame, and Lisa Pearce, assistant professor of sociology at the University of North Carolina at Chapel Hill.

Moreover, sociological research shows a strong correlation between religiously active families and positive outcomes for children on a wide range of issues, such as helpfulness, drug use, self-image, and life attitudes, among others. Even children who attend religious education classes at church do not do as well as children whose parents also practice and teach their faith at home. (For a summary of the research, read "Best Practices in Family Faith Formation," by John Roberto, available online, or visit the website of the National Study on Youth and Religion at youthandreligion.nd.edu.)

These research findings only confirm what the Church has known for generations: When we respond to God's call, good things happen.

What do the icons mean?

The icons for each article allow you to quickly find the prayer practices that are most appropriate for your family.

(**e**) These are prayer practices that are easy to do immediately, without any prior preparation.

3+ These practices are appropriate for children between ages three and six.

7+ These practices are appropriate for children between ages seven to twelve.

13+ These practices are appropriate for teens.

Does our family need to do all of these prayer practices?

Definitely not! Most Catholic families are doing well if they make a habit of just a handful of these practices.

The idea behind this book is to provide families with a menu of different Catholic practices to try. Some items will become regular features in your family life, while others you might try only once or twice.

That said, you might make it your goal to at least try most of these practices. Even if some don't work out for your family right now, your children may remember the practice later in life, when it might be just the right fit.

How do I find time to pray with my kids?

One of the purposes of this book is to provide you with a wide variety of strategies so that you can find a handful that will fit into your family's busy schedule. See, in particular, the ideas listed under the **Times to Pray Together** chapter.

Family researcher Loren D. Marks, co-author of the textbook *Sacred Matters: Religion and Spirituality in Families* (Routledge, 2011), observes that family rituals require structure, effort, organization, and flexibility within families, and that modern families "often struggle to maintain even the most meaningful and sacred of practices because of the competing challenges of life from outside forces."

Marks notes two strategies common to families who regularly practice their faith together. First, these families set aside regular "sacred time" for faith-based activities—often the same time of day (such as before meals) or the same time each week (a Friday evening or Sunday morning). Second, these families continue setting aside time for shared faith activities despite occasional resistance from their children or the dominant culture. And key to their persistence is their understanding that these sacred family practices are not always going to be (and do not always need to be) perfect.

How do I teach my kids to be quiet, respectful, and reverent during prayer?

You can and should set high expectations for your kids' attitude and behavior during prayer, but don't expect to see that behavior right away.

The good news is that hundreds of generations of parents have faced the same challenges before you; most of them report that the messiness of praying with kids does get better over time.

In the meantime, it is okay for your family prayer time to be less than perfect. Even when it is frustrating, the very act of trying to pray is itself a prayer, a striving toward God.

For some practical tips on how to survive the prayer-time crazies, see the related discussion under the Family Prayer Time article.

What is Peanut Butter & Grace and pbgrace.com?

Peanut Butter & Grace is a project devoted to promoting and supporting home-based Catholic family faith formation. The name is a whimsical reference to the venerable peanut butter and jelly sandwich, that staple of kids' lunches (at least in the U.S.). Nutritious, delicious, easy to make, and a little bit messy—just like the family faith formation activities promoted by Peanut Butter & Grace.

At pbgrace.com, you can look up the articles in this book for links to additional online resources, or to leave comments about your own ideas and experiences. You'll also find articles from the other books in Peanut Butter & Grace Guides for Catholic Families series, as well as bonus articles not found in the books.

Who wrote this book?

Allow me an introduction: I'm Jerry Windley-Daoust, the father of five children who range in age from four to fourteen (at the time of this writing). For the past ten years or so, I've spent most of my days changing diapers, making peanut butter and jelly sandwiches, and slinging babies (in a baby sling, not in a slingshot) while my wife taught theology at Saint Mary's University. I maintained my sanity (mostly) and probably became a better dad by participating in the parent education classes offered by our local school district, as well as my parish's prayer and study group for stay-at-home parents. Over the years, I was privileged to swap war stories and practical wisdom with hundreds of stay-at-home moms (and a few dads) in these groups, and I've woven some of that wisdom into these pages.

Before my days as a wrangler of kids, I used my background in journalism and pastoral ministry as an editor of high school catechetical textbooks for Saint Mary's Press.

Where did the ideas in this book come from?

As you might guess, many of the ideas and insights in this book come from my own experience as a stay-at-home dad, as well as the experiences of other moms and dads from my parenting groups. In addition, I have tapped into research on the religious formation of children and adolescents, some of which is mentioned above.

The faith content of this book draws heavily on the *Catechism of the Catholic Church*, especially "Part Four: Christian Prayer." Because this is a practical guide and not a faith formation textbook, you will need to go to the *Catechism* or other catechetical resources to learn more about particular practices; where appropriate, I have provided citations for this purpose.

Finally, I am also indebted to *Catholic Household Blessings and Prayers*, which is published by the U.S. Catholic bishops (USCCB Publishing, 2007). While there are many other fine Catholic prayer books available, *Catholic Household Blessings and Prayers* has the advantage of including numerous blessings from the Church's official *Book of Blessings* that have been adapted for home use. In addition, it is a comprehensive and well-rounded resource, including not only most traditional Catholic prayers, but also prayers that express the needs of the modern world.

What else can I do to nurture the faith of my children?

In "Best Practices in Family Faith Formation," John Roberto identifies several recurring themes in the research literature on the faith lives of children and families. These themes point to five "core practices" that, "if consistently acted upon at home and supported by congregations, would contribute to building families of faithful Christians. . . ." Those practices include:

- Having conversations that connect faith and daily life, and studying the faith together

- Praying together, both at home and with the Church

- Serving others together

- Maintaining family rituals, traditions, and celebrations

- Eating meals together

This book addresses the second of those core practices.

CHAPTER ONE

How to Pray Together

By reason of their dignity and mission,
Christian parents have the specific responsibility
of educating their children in prayer, introducing
them to gradual discovery of the mystery of
God and to personal dialogue with Him.

—Pope John Paul II, *On the Role of the Christian Family in the Modern World*, 60

Prayer is essential to the Christian life, and parents are the primary people responsible for teaching their children to pray. But if you've ever tried to pray with a four-year-old who won't stop jumping on the bed, or a resentful teenager who has better things to do, then your first reaction might just be, "Easier said than done!" And the task is doubly daunting for those of us whose prayer life isn't what we'd like it to be (which is most of us).

This book aims to help you pray with your kids by offering you a wide variety of styles and strategies from the long tradition of Christian prayer. But before we begin to look at different ways of praying with our kids, it might be good to pause a moment to ask: Just what it is we're trying to do here? What does it mean to "pray" with our kids?

What Is Prayer?

Whole libraries of books have been written in response to the questions, "What is prayer?" and "How do I pray?" But the *Catechism of the Catholic Church* offers a simple enough definition at the beginning of its fourth part, "Christian Prayer." Prayer, it says, is "a vital and personal relationship with the living and true God" (2558). We hear this definition echoed in Pope John Paul II's statement, quoted above, that Christian parents should introduce their children "to gradual discovery of the mystery of God and to personal dialogue with Him" through prayer.

If prayer is a relationship and a dialogue with God, then teaching our children to pray isn't like teaching them to ride a bike or to do calculus. It is much more like teaching them how to be friends with someone . . . except that in this case, the "someone" also happens to be the source and ground of their very being.

The experience of holy men and women throughout the ages offers other helpful insights into the nature of prayer. Consider the following reflections by these widely acknowledged masters of Christian prayer:

> St. Thérèse of Lisieux: "For me, prayer is a surge of the heart; it is a simple look turned toward heaven, it is a cry of recognition and of love."

> St. Theresa of Avila: "Mental prayer is, as I see it, simply a friendly intercourse, and frequent solitary conversation with Him who, as we know, loves us."

> Pope John XXIII: "Prayer is the raising of the mind to God. We must always remember this. The actual words matter less."

St. Basil the Great: "The best form of prayer is one that . . . makes space for the presence of God within us."

St. John Climacus: "Prayer is by nature a dialogue and a union of man with God; its effect is to hold the world together, for it achieves a reconciliation with God."

St. Theophan the Recluse: "Whoever has passed through actions and thought to true feeling, will pray without words, for God is God of the heart."

Clement of Alexandria: "Even if we speak with a low voice, even if we whisper without opening the lips, even if we call to him only from the depths of our heart, our unspoken word always reaches God, and God always listens."

This, then, is the far horizon that we are aiming for when we pray with our kids. Helping our kids to memorize a handful of prayers and to recite those prayers at mealtime and bedtime is a great place to start, but it is not our kids' ultimate destination. Ultimately, they are called to a life illuminated by the presence of God.

Leading Children to God through Prayer

If that description of prayer leaves you more daunted than encouraged, consider three points that might make the responsibility of educating your children in prayer a little less overwhelming.

1. The Holy Spirit Is Already at Work in Your Child

It is the Holy Spirit who teaches us how to pray (see Luke 11:13; Romans 8:26). The Holy Spirit is already at work in your child, simply by virtue of his baptism. Even if your child hasn't been baptized, as one created in the image of God, his deepest self longs for God. That longing may be hard to see, but it's there; it's a fundamental fact of human nature. And even if your child actively turns away from God, God will never stop seeking him out (*CCC*, 27, 30).

So while parents may be responsible for "introducing" their children to the mystery of God through prayer, it is the Holy Spirit who ultimately leads each person to God. As St. Paul says: "I planted, Apollos watered, but God gave the growth. So neither the one who plants nor the one who waters is anything, but only God who gives the growth" (1 Corinthians 3:6–7).

As you pray with your kids, learn to recognize the Holy Spirit at work in them—and, when necessary, get out of the way.

2. The Holy Spirit Is at Work in You, Too

Besides trusting the work of the Holy Spirit in your child, you can also trust that the same Spirit is at work in you. Even if your own prayer life is far from perfect, God will use whatever you have to help your child grow in faith.

3. The Community of Believers Has Your Back

The main way that the Holy Spirit teaches people to pray is "through the believing and praying Church" (*CCC*, 2650). From the Israelites gathered with Moses at the base of Mount Sinai to the disciples gathered in the upper room and beyond, prayer has always been the work of the whole community of believers. And it is the whole community of believers that hands on the tradition of prayer.

In other words, teaching your child to pray isn't something you have to do by yourself; you have the help of the whole Church. What does this mean, practically speaking? For starters, if you do nothing more than take your children to Mass, the sacraments, and other liturgical celebrations, you've already laid a solid foundation for a vibrant prayer life. The prayer of the community—what the Church calls *liturgy*—is one of the most important ways children learn to pray (see *CCC*, 1074–1075).

But it also means that the incredible wealth of the Church's long tradition of prayer—the wisdom of the saints, the mystics, and the whole People of God (including lots of moms and dads just like you)—is at your disposal. You don't need to reinvent the wheel!

Getting Started

Here are a few practical tips to consider as you begin exploring different ways of praying with your kids:

Start out small. Choose the simplest, easiest practices and work your way up to more involved ones. Want to dig deeper? Find these articles on pbgrace.com and follow the links to additional resources.

Try out one idea at a time. If it works, try making it a regular part of your family's "prayer menu"; if it doesn't, move on.

Try out a variety of different prayer styles. Even if a particular practice doesn't suit your children now, they might return to that way of praying later in life.

Make a few prayer practices a family habit. If you manage to incorporate even a handful of these practices into your family life on a regular basis, you will be doing great.

"Unless You Become Like Children . . . "

A final thought: Praying with our kids isn't a one-way street. It isn't only we, as parents, who introduce our kids to the mystery of God; if we are attentive, our kids can lead us deeper into the mystery of God, too.

When you pause in your busy life to pray with your kids, then, hold in your heart these words of Jesus:

> At that time the disciples came to Jesus and asked,
> "Who is the greatest in the kingdom of heaven?"
> He called a child, whom he put among them, and
> said, "Truly I tell you, unless you change and become
> like children, you will never enter the kingdom of
> heaven. Whoever becomes humble like this child
> is the greatest in the kingdom of heaven. Whoever
> welcomes one such child in my name welcomes me."
> (Matthew 18:1–5)

CHAPTER TWO

Times to Pray Together

Baby Prayers

You don't need to wait for your children to talk to begin teaching them how to pray. In fact, you can begin right away, in those first magical moments after your child is born and in the days and weeks that follow, by using the ordinary tasks of caring for your baby (diaper changes, feedings, and so on) as prompts to prayer.

Admittedly, praying with your baby is an indirect way to teach him or her how to pray. On the other hand, infants and toddlers are great imitators, and more tuned in to their parents than at any other time in their lives. If you make it a habit to pray with your child out loud, with sign language, or even by pausing to adopt a quiet, prayerful attitude, the day will come when you find your child trying to mimic your actions and words.

Even more importantly, when you pray with your baby, you intentionally open yourself to the presence of God—and there is no better place for you and your baby to be.

Laura Kelly Fanucci, the author of the popular Catholic blog Mothering Spirit, has written a beautiful series on praying with your baby. The following suggestions about when and how to pray with your baby are adapted from a few of her ideas:

Feeding. As you feed your child, think of all the good meals you have enjoyed throughout your life, and give thanks. Think in particular about all those who have fed you over the years (parents, grandparents, and others) and give thanks for them. Pray for your child to be fed by God, and to have a generous heart that feeds others, especially those who are most vulnerable.

Cleaning up. As you change diapers or wash your spit-up-stained clothes, ask Mary (who changed a few diapers in her time) to help you care for your child with the same tenderness with which she cared for the baby Jesus.

Waking in the night. The next time you have to wake up in the middle of the night for your baby, remember the monastic practice of waking in the middle of the night to pray the **Liturgy of the Hours**; make this time your own Liturgy of the Hours. Think of all the other people awake in the night—police and doctors and bakers, people in crisis, and those unable to sleep because of worry or medical problems—and pray for them. Pray in thanksgiving for God, who is always "awake," watching over us.

Crying. When baby won't stop crying (or screaming), remember all those around the world crying out for help, or crying in distress. Remember especially the many children whose cries will go unanswered, and offer up your own small burden in prayer for them. Ask the Holy Spirit to help you care for your child lovingly, just as God cares for us in our own distress.

You can find expanded versions of these ideas and many others at Mothering Spirit; find the link by looking up this article at pbgrace.com.

Bedtime Prayers

Right before bed is often a good time to have a short family prayer service; see **Family Prayer Time** for ideas and suggestions.

If you prefer, you can have your children pray a short prayer in (or kneeling next to) their beds. Check out **A Handful of Catholic Prayers** at the back of this book for some children's bedtime prayers; older kids and teens may prefer to pray some of the evening prayers from the **Liturgy of Hours**.

Here are some other ideas for simple ways to pray with a child at her bedside; refer to the boldfaced articles for more details:

- Bless your child, and let him bless you; see **Bless One Another**.

- Do a kid-friendly **Daily Examen**.

- Talk about the day's **Highs and Lows**, using them to launch a short, spontaneous prayer.

- Keep a small picture of Jesus, Mary, or the angels where your child can see it from bed. (You can also purchase religiously themed nightlights.)

- Read a Bible story and use it to launch a short prayer. The *Catholic Book of Bible Stories* by Laurie Lazzaro Knowlton (Zonderkidz, 2004) includes a brief prayer at the end of each story.

- Sing a kid-friendly religious song from a hymnal or an album of religious children's songs. See **Sing Your Prayer**.

- Make a **Prayer Pillowcase** for your child's pillow.

- Use **Grab-Bag Prayers** to help your child pick friends and relatives to pray for.

- Pray a modified, kid-friendly version of the rosary; see **Pray the Rosary**.

- Use the five forms of prayer outlined in the *Catechism of the Catholic Church* (see **Pray the Five Forms of Prayer**) or Pope Francis's Five-Finger Prayer (find it in **A Handful of Catholic Prayers**) as a guide for your bedtime prayers.

- Keep a **Prayer Journal** or **Gratitude or Thanksgiving Journal** by your child's bedside for writing down her prayers; see **Write Your Prayers** for more ideas.

- Read the story of a saint and use it to pray for the saint's intercession (see **Saint Prayers**). The *Once Upon a Time Saints* series by Ethel Pochocki (Bethlehem Books, 1996) make wonderful bedtime stories.

- Keep a list of prayer intentions and use them to guide bedtime prayers (see **List Your Prayer Intentions**).

- Recite traditional Catholic prayers such as the Our Father, Hail Mary, the Prayer to St. Michael, the Canticle of Mary, etc. (See **Pray Traditional Prayers and Devotions**.) If you recite one or more of these prayers slowly every night, most children old enough to talk will eventually join in.

Evening Prayer

Evening Prayer is one of the "major hours" of the Liturgy of the Hours that the Church prays throughout the day. If you don't do **Family Prayer Time** in the evening, try to incorporate some sort of evening prayer ritual into your end-of-day routine. Check out the **Liturgy of the Hours** article for more information about Evening Prayer, or find some simple evening prayers you can use in **A Handful of Catholic Prayers**.

With younger children, try some of the ideas listed under **Bedtime Prayers**.

Finally, these Scriptural prayers may also be used as part of your Evening Prayer:

Psalm 141:1-9 ("I have called to you, Lord. . . .")

Psalm 142 ("With all my voice I cry to the Lord. . . .")

Philippians 2:6-11 ("Though he was in the form of God. . . .").

Family Prayer Time

Set aside a regular time to pray together as a family—or, if your schedules don't allow for the whole family to pray together, aim to pray together one-on-one or in small groups.

Tips for Getting Started

Find a regular time to pray, and make it a habit. Your family prayer time might be daily, or once a week (Sunday afternoons or Wednesday evenings, for example). Psychologists say that it can take months of persistence to develop a habit. You can help the process along by hooking family prayer to another family habit. Do your younger kids already have a bedtime routine? Kick it off by sitting down together for prayer. Does your family eat meals together? Work in a short time of prayer at the beginning and end of the meal. The time before Sunday Mass, driving to school, watching TV, brushing teeth—any of these activities might be a trigger for shared prayer.

Start small. Until family prayer time is a habit, you may need to start small. If you can't do a ten-minute prayer service, start with five; if you can't do five minutes, start with sixty seconds, or even a ten-second blessing on the way out the door in the morning.

Find a style of prayer that fits your family now. Try out different prayer practices until you find one that works for your family at this time in your kids' faith development. You will find many ideas in the rest of this book, especially in the **Ways of Praying Together** chapter.

Let kids lead. Giving kids choices, input, and leadership opportunities is a great way to get them engaged, and also prepares them to pray on their own initiative. See **Let Kids Lead** for ideas.

Coping with the Prayer-Time Crazies

Praying with kids can be more messy than holy, especially when you are just beginning to pray together, and especially when young children are involved. Know that you are not alone: hundreds of generations of Christian parents have had the same experience. Is your toddler using the rosary as a slingshot? Been there and done that. Does your teen pray through gritted teeth? Check. Is your second grader kicking your ten-year-old as you pray the Our Father? At least they're not actually killing one another, which is more than could be said about Cain and Abel during *their* family prayer time (see Genesis 4:1–9).

Here are some tips for dealing with the prayer-time crazies:

Pray now, discipline later. Unless kids are in danger of getting hurt or destroying property, ignore their behavior and focus on your own prayer (you'll need the extra grace anyway). If you constantly stop praying to deal with their behavior, then they are running the show—and you're no longer praying. You can discuss expectations and hand out consequences after prayer is done.

Start out small. Begin by making family prayer time just as long as you can tolerate your kids' behavior. You may even need to begin by simply sprinkling some five-second Invocations throughout your day.

Stick with it to establish new expectations. Kids are often resistant to new routines or changes in expectations. Stick with it through the initial resistance. As prayer becomes a habit and regular expectation, and as you find the prayer practices that best fit your family, you will begin seeing the fruits of your efforts.

Explain why you're praying. If your kids ask questions about why you're praying (or praying in a new way), offer them a brief explanation; you can use the **Talking Points** section of many articles in this book as a starting point.

Be patient. Sometimes you will think, "We didn't actually pray; we just went through the motions." Although it may not *feel* rewarding, sometimes going through the motions is prayer nonetheless, because it is its own kind of striving toward God. And one day, you and your kids will be "just going through the motions" and discover yourselves surrounded by the presence of God.

Learn More
Acts 2:46
CCC, 2685
On the Role of the Christian Family in the Modern World (Familiaris Consortio), 59–62

Go on a Pilgrimage

Consider working a pilgrimage into your next day trip or family vacation.

A pilgrimage is a journey to a holy place that the traveler undertakes for spiritual growth. By going to the holy place, the pilgrim hopes to enter more fully into the presence of God. The journey itself is marked by prayer, charitable works, hospitality toward fellow travelers, and an attitude that any hardships encountered along the way are opportunities for spiritual growth.

There are literally thousands of Christian pilgrimage sites around the world . . . places where people have encountered God in a special way. Chances are good that there is a site near you or your vacation destination. Just a handful of pilgrimage possibilities include:

St. John Paul II National Shrine. Visitors to this shrine in Washington, D.C., can also view exhibits on the life of Pope John Paul II and the history of Catholics in America.

National Shrine of Our Lady of the Snows. Located in Belleville, Illinois, this shrine features a variety of devotional areas, including a Children's Memorial Playground, Annunciation Garden, Mother's Prayer Walk, and more.

El Santuario de Chimayó. This shrine in Chimayó, New Mexico, receives up to 300,000 visitors a year, and is famous for the healing power of its dirt.

National Shrine of Our Lady of Guadalupe. Located in La Crosse, Wisconsin, this shrine includes a rosary walk, Stations of the Cross walk, and Our Lady of Good Counsel Votive Chapel among its devotional areas.

European pilgrimage sites. Europe is littered with pilgrimage sites, the most famous of which are Lourdes (France), Fatima (Portugal), Assisi (Italy), and of course St. Peter's Basilica (the Vatican).

World Youth Day. Hundreds of thousands of youth and young adults gather with the pope and other Catholic leaders during World Youth Day, which is held in a different country every three years. For a closer alternative, look into national youth festivals such as the National Catholic Youth Conference (in the United States), the Australian Catholic Youth Festival, or the Youth 2000 Summer Festival (Ireland).

The Holy Land. A visit to the places featured in the Gospel is a once-in-a-lifetime pilgrimage.

You can find more pilgrimage sites by searching "Catholic pilgrimage" online; add the name of your state or city to find local sites. If you can't find a widely recognized pilgrimage site that you can visit, you can choose another destination that has some spiritual significance: a cathedral or basilica, for instance; places associated with a saint or holy person; or a museum exhibit of religious art.

Learn More
CCC, 2691

Liturgy of the Hours

St. Paul urged the earliest Christians to "pray constantly" (1 Thessalonians 5:17). Over the centuries, the Church developed a way to help people, especially clerics and religious, to pray at regular intervals throughout the day. This traditional practice is known as the Liturgy of the Hours, or Divine Office. The prayers associated with the Liturgy of the Hours center around psalms and canticles from the Scriptures, and are devised so that "the whole course of the day and night is made holy by the praise of God" (*CCC*, 1174); they are like an extension of the celebration of Mass into everyday life.

Pope John Paul II reaffirmed the call of the Second Vatican Council for families to pray the Liturgy of the Hours together (*Familiaris Consortio*, 61). If you'd like to try praying the Liturgy of the Hours with your family, you'll either need to purchase a book containing the official prayers (called a breviary) or find a resource adapting those prayers for use by the laity. You can find links to both options at pbgrace.com.

Even if your family doesn't pray all of the official prayers every three hours, it offers a good launching point for a daily devotional practice. See **Morning Prayer**, **Noon Prayer**, and **Evening Prayer** for some simple options for praying during the "major hours" of the day.

Learn More
CCC, 1174–1178

Mealtime Prayers

You'll find a number of mealtime prayers in **A Handful of Catholic Prayers** at the end of this book. Here are some other ideas for praying mealtime prayers:

Start with silence. Try **Thirty Seconds of Silence** before saying your mealtime prayer together.

Bless your family. Besides blessing the food, you can also ask for God's blessing on your family and your conversation. (If your meals are fraught and chaotic affairs, all the more reason to pray for help!)

Pray after the meal. Some people also pray after the meal. If you try this, you can either pray together before everyone is excused, or encourage kids to make the Sign of the Cross before they leave the table.

Offer a menu of prayers. Use Table Triangles as aids to learning new mealtime prayers, and to give kids a choice of mealtime prayers to say.

Let kids lead. Mealtime prayers are an excellent time to let kids begin leading prayer. (See the related article, "**Let Kids Lead**.")

Sacred reading. In some monasteries, meals are eaten in silence while one of the monks or nuns reads some sacred text. You can adapt this practice by reading the day's Scripture readings before, during, or after your meal.

For a fine collection of creative mealtime prayers for many different types of food and times of year, see *Peanut Butter and Jelly Prayers* by Julie B. Sevig (Morehouse Publishing, 2007).

Talking Points: Why Do We Pray Before Meals?

Christians (and people from most other religious traditions) pray before they eat as a way of thanking God for their food. For most of human history (and for too many people today), regular meals were never guaranteed. Blessing food reminds us that all good things—including the food on our table and the life it sustains—ultimately come from God.

Learn More

CCC, 2834

Morning Prayer

When you wake up, offer your day to God in one of the following ways:

Morning Offering. Say the traditional Morning Offering prayer (see **A Handful of Catholic Prayers**).

Invocations. Not a morning person? Keep it short by memorizing a handful of one-line invocations to pray in the morning (see some examples in the related article, **Invocations**).

Canticle of Zechariah. The Canticle of Zechariah is one of the traditional morning prayers of the Liturgy of the Hours, possibly because Zechariah's song (found in Luke 1:68–79) refers to Christ as the dawn. (You can find the full text in **A Handful of Catholic Prayers**.)

Sing a song. You can sing "This Is the Day the Lord Has Made" or another popular morning hymn.

Pray a psalm. Psalms often prayed during Morning Prayer include Psalm 63:2–9 ("O God, you are my God; for you I long. . . ."), Daniel 3:57–88 ("Bless the Lord, all you works of the Lord. . . .") and Psalm 149 ("Sing a new song to the Lord. . . .").

Write your prayer. If singing morning prayer gets you dirty looks from family members, try writing out your morning prayer and leaving it in a prominent place: on the refrigerator, on a closet door, on the bathroom mirror.

Post your prayer. Teens who use social media might make a morning offering their first post of the day.

Noon Prayer

If you are trying to pray an adapted form of the **Liturgy of the Hours** as a family, incorporate some form of noon or midday prayer into your routine.

In *Catholic Household Blessings and Prayers* (USCCB Publishing, 2007), the U.S. Catholic bishops recommend reciting the Angelus ("The angel of the Lord declared unto Mary. . .") or, during Easter, the Regina Caeli ("Queen of Heaven, rejoice, alleluia. . .") at noon. Both are centuries-old prayers with monastic roots; you can find both in **A Handful of Catholic Prayers** at the back of this book. You can also pray the prayers prescribed by the **Liturgy of the Hours** for noon.

Other ideas for praying noon prayer with younger children:

Teach classic mealtime prayers. Use lunchtime to help your kids memorize classic Mealtime Prayers, with the promise that when they have mastered the prayer, they will be able to lead the family in prayer at dinnertime.

Sing your prayer. Make a ritual of playing a favorite Christian song before you eat lunch. Try to learn the words so you and your children can sing along. (You might try doing this while preparing lunch as a way of keeping the kids occupied.)

Pray the Scriptures with little helpers. If you have a little helper assisting you with lunch preparations, tell him stories of meals in the Gospels, and use those stories as a starting point for a spontaneous mealtime prayer. Some possibilities include the story of the multiplication of the loaves and fishes (especially the version in John 6:1–14, in which a boy shares his lunch); the resurrected Jesus sharing breakfast with his disciples on a beach (see John 21:1–14); and Jesus coming to dinner at the home of Zacchaeus (see Luke 19:1–10). You can also imagine together how Mary made lunch for Jesus.

Pray Before School

Send your kids off to school with a quick prayer.

At the door. Keep it simple by blessing one another as you go out the door, or offer a simple one-line prayer: "May God bless you and keep you, all the day long." (See **Bless One Another**.)

In the car. If you drive your kids to school and they are old enough to read, give one of them a prayer book and ask him to choose a prayer to read on the way. If you have time, ask for prayer intentions for the day (for tests, presentations, sick classmates, etc.).

At the flagpole. If your church or community sponsors a See You At the Pole prayer event at your school's flagpole (usually the fourth Wednesday of September), consider participating.

Pray Comings and Goings

When a member of your family will be away from home for a while (a first sleepover, a military deployment, college, business trip, camp, etc.), mark their departure with prayers for their safety and well-being, and their return with prayers of gratitude and celebration. You can find such prayers in Catholic Household Blessings and Prayers, or pray spontaneously. For especially significant absences, plan a simple prayer service. You can include music, appropriate Scripture readings, blessings, and environmental elements such as candles (see **Smells and Bells**).

Pray for Emergency Vehicles

When you hear an emergency vehicle's siren, say a short prayer for the emergency responders and the people they are going to help. You can pray an Our Father, or even something as simple as, "God, please be with the people who are scared and needing help; please be with the emergency helpers to keep them safe and to help them to know what to do." Close with the Sign of the Cross.

Talking Points: The Power of Prayer
You can point out to your children that God wants us to help those in need—personally, with our own hands, if possible. (You

can tell them the parable of the Good Samaritan, found in Luke 10:25–37.) However, when it is impossible to help someone personally, God gives us the opportunity to reach out to people in need through our prayer. When we pray for those in need, we participate in God's work in their lives.

Learn More
CCC, 2634–2636

Pray Life Events

"We must pray without ceasing, in every occurrence and employment in our lives," said St. Elizabeth Ann Seton, a mother of five children (*Collected Writings*, Vincentian Digital Books). One way to do that is by pausing to pray in response to the events in our lives, both ordinary and extraordinary. The prayer can be very simple (a sentence or even a short phrase), or more formal and involved.

This book provides some ideas for life events that might become prompts for prayer (see, for example, **Baby Prayers, Evening Prayer, Morning Prayer, Pray for the Sick, Pray for Emergency Vehicles, Pray Before School, Pray Comings and Goings**).

Catholic Household Blessings and Prayers provides additional ideas for occasions of prayer and blessings, including: birthdays, addiction, moving, childbirth, miscarriage, adoption, nursing or feeding a child, baptismal anniversary, graduation, engagement to be married, wedding anniversary, leaving home (for an extended period of time), retirement, work, study, travel, welcoming guests, beginning or ending a school year, unemployment, planting, harvesting, sports events, the blessing of objects (such as tools, art materials, products of nature, family vehicle, home), neighborhood or family strife, financial difficulties, weather, and discernment.

The bottom line? "Praying constantly" means recognizing God's presence in each and every moment of our lives—and consciously responding to that presence in our words and actions as often as we are able.

Pray When You Pass a Church

An old Catholic tradition is the practice of saying a quick prayer—typically the Sign of the Cross or a short exhortation such as "Jesus, we love you!"—when passing a Catholic church, in acknowledgement of Jesus' real presence in the form of the Eucharist in the church's tabernacle. See **Eucharistic Adoration** for some talking points related to this practice.

Retreat in Prayer

Jesus frequently went off by himself to pray, away from the crowds and the disciples and his usual routine. Throughout the centuries, Christians have sought to renew and deepen their faith by retreating to a quiet place to rest, pray, and be in the presence of God.

Here are some ideas for incorporating a prayer retreat into your own family life:

Retreat once a year. Try to get away on a retreat at least once a year. If possible, go on retreat with your spouse; otherwise, take turns (one goes on retreat while the other takes care of the kids). An annual retreat might seem impossible to fit into your busy schedule, but you will almost certainly find the benefits to be worth the extra time.

Retreat centers. Find a retreat center near your home. Retreat centers usually offer group retreats (mixing talks and group reflection with individual quiet time) as well as individual directed or self-directed retreats. Directed retreats involve meeting with a spiritual director; self-directed retreats are done on one's own, perhaps with the guidance of a retreat book. Retreat centers usually offer simple but quiet accommodations, a place to pray, and a beautiful natural environment, at an affordable cost.

Parish retreats. Participate in retreats sponsored by your parish, and encourage your teens to participate as well.

Family retreats. If you have older children or teens, consider going on a family retreat. A handful of Catholic retreat centers offer retreats designed for families; you'll find links to some of them at pbgrace.com.

Retreat at home. Alternatively, you can do a family retreat at home using any of the many books offering guidance for self-directed retreats; see pbgrace.com for examples, or search "busy person's retreat" or "daily retreat" online.

Work as Prayer

Help your kids develop a Christian attitude toward work by teaching them how to make their work—whether around the house or at school—into a prayer:

Talk to kids about the Christian attitude toward work. See the *Talking Points* section below for a brief summary of the Christian tradition around work. With older children or teens, read or summarize the relevant sections of the *Catechism of the Catholic Church*, the *Compendium of the Social Doctrine of the Church*, or the writings of the saints.

Begin chores with a short prayer. Attitude and intention are key elements of prayerful work. Help set the right mood by beginning your chore time with a very brief prayer. *Catholic Household Blessings and Prayers* contains several blessings of work. Or, read an excerpt from the first creation account in the Book of Genesis: "God saw everything that he had made, and indeed, it was very good. . . . Thus the heavens and the earth were finished, and all their multitude. And on the seventh day God finished the work that he had done, and he rested on the seventh day from all the work that he had done" (Genesis 1:31—2:2).

Play music during chore time. As anyone who has ever watched *Snow White* knows, a little music makes any chore go faster.

Prayerfully reflect on your work. Incorporate your family's work into a **Daily Examen**, or make Genesis chapters 1 and 2 (the creation stories) the subject of a **Lectio Divina** meditation on human work as a participation in God's work of creation.

Take pictures of kids' work to offer to God. Make the idea of offering our work to God more concrete for younger children by taking pictures of them doing their chores (or of the completed work). Print out the pictures and write, "Father, I offer you this work of my hands" on it. Then place it in **God's Mailbox** or your **Home Oratory**, or in the collection basket during the Offertory at Mass.

Talking Points: A Christian Attitude Toward Work

While Greek and Roman culture typically regarded human labor as debasing—a necessary evil relegated to the lower social classes—the early Christians, drawing on their Jewish roots, saw work as another way for people to connect with God. Work that orders even a small corner of the world toward beauty and the common good is a sort of participation in God's ongoing work of creation, the Church says: "Human work, directed to charity as its final goal, becomes an occasion for contemplation; it becomes devout prayer..." (*Compendium of the Social Doctrine of the Church, 266*).

This attitude toward work has been developed and nurtured over the centuries in monasteries, where work is an integral part of the daily routine. Brother Lawrence of the Resurrection's *The Practice of the Presence of God* and St. Thérèse of Lisieux's "Little Way" are just two of many examples of methods that elevate even menial work to God.

Learn More

CCC, 2427–2428
Compendium of the Social Doctrine of the Church, 255–322

CHAPTER THREE

Ways of Praying Together

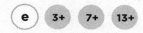

Answer the Questions Jesus Asks

The Bible records hundreds of questions that Jesus posed to his listeners—questions that continue to call for a response from his followers even today.

Make the questions of Jesus a launching point for prayer and reflection with older children and teens, using the method of **Lectio Divina**. Here are a few questions to consider:

> "Can any of you by worrying add a single moment to your life?" (Matthew 6:27; Luke 12:26)

> "Why are you afraid, you of little faith?" (Matthew 8:26)

> "Do you believe that I am able to do this?" (Matthew 9:28)

> "Why did you doubt?" (Matthew 14:31)

> "Who do people say that I am? . . . But who do you say that I am?" (Matthew 16:13, 15)

"What do you want me to do for you?"
(Matthew 20:32; Mark 10:36, 51; Luke 18:41)

"Are your hearts hardened? Do you have eyes, and
fail to see? Do you have ears, and fail to hear? And do
you not remember?" (Mark 8:17–18)

"Why do you raise such questions in your hearts?"
(Luke 5:22)

"Why do you call me 'Lord, Lord,' and do not do what
I tell you?" (Luke 6:46)

"What is your name?" (Luke 8:30)

"Why are you frightened, and why do doubts arise in
your hearts?" (Luke 24:38)

"What are you looking for?" (John 1:38)

"Do you want to be made well?" (John 5:6)

"Do you know what I have done to you?" (John 13:12)

"Do you love me?" (John 21:16)

"Why do you persecute me?" (Acts 9:4)

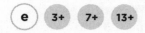

Ask for What You Need

Here is a very simple and effective way to pray: When you or your children need help—especially when you need spiritual help—ask for it in prayer.

You can make your prayer simple and straightforward: "Holy Spirit, give me patience—because right now I'm out of it!" Or you can ask for it as part of a longer prayer that begins with praise and ends with thanksgiving and gratitude. (See **Pray the Five Forms of Prayer**.)

Model this form of prayer (called a petition) by praying out loud for what you need right in the moment, and by encouraging kids to pray for what they need as well:

* for help mastering a skill;

* for wisdom, patience, courage, or other virtues needed to handle a difficult situation;

* for peace following a tragedy;

* for small daily needs, from finding a parking spot to getting homework done;

* for finding lost objects (Catholics traditionally ask St. Anthony to pray with them for this).

Be sure to tell your kids that while God always answers our prayers, he always does so in a way that is best for us and others involved in our situation; see the ***Talking Points*** section below.

Talking Points: Asking God for What We Need

In the Gospels, all of the people who requested help from Jesus did so quite simply. Consider Peter, sinking into the waves of the raging sea: "Lord, save me!" (Matthew 14:30). Or consider the healing of two blind men. Hearing that Jesus is approaching, they call to him: "Have mercy on us, Lord, Son of David!" The crowd "sternly orders" them to be quiet. Instead, they call all the louder. Hearing them, Jesus stops and asks, "What do you want me to do for you?" "Lord," they reply, "let our eyes be opened." Jesus, "filled with compassion," touches their eyes and heals them (paraphrased from Matthew 20:29–34.)

Jesus poses the same question to each of us: "What do you want me to do for you?" And he assures us that we will receive whatever "good things" we ask for in prayer (Matthew 7:7).

Sometimes kids (and adults!) regard prayer as magic, or God as a sort of vending machine that sometimes works and sometimes doesn't. But when Jesus promises that the Father will give us whatever good things we ask for, he does so in the context of the relationship between a parent and a child: "Is there anyone among you who, if your child asks for bread, will give a stone? Or if the child asks for a fish, will give a snake?" (Matthew 7:9–10). Conversely, if a child asks for a (presumably poisonous) snake, the caring parent will say no, or offer something else. So it is with God.

Older kids and teens can especially be encouraged to focus their petitionary prayer on spiritual goods (humility, a generous heart, the strength to forgive, etc.). Such prayers are most likely to be answered directly and abundantly—although in God's time, and sometimes in ways that surprise us.

At the same time, God *wants* us to come to him with our needs in prayer, and no request is too small or trivial. Remember that Jesus helped Peter and his friends catch fish, changed water into wine to keep a party going, and listened compassionately to Martha's request for help with housework. In Martha's case, of course, he answered her petition in a different way than she expected, which just goes to show that even if our prayer isn't answered the way we would like, God uses our request to help us grow closer to him.

Learn More
Matthew 7:7-11; John 9:10
CCC, 2629–2633

Bite-Sized Biblical Prayers

The Bible is replete with prayers you can adapt for **Family Prayer Time**. The psalms are a rich source, of course, but there are prayers and canticles (songs) scattered throughout the Bible. You can either read these as part of your prayer time, or meditate on them through repetition or the method of **Lectio Divina**.

Even single lines of Scripture may be adapted to prayer. These bite-sized verses are perfect for children, who can memorize them so they will always have a quick devotional prayer handy (see **Memorizing Prayers**).

Biblical Prayers to Use with Kids
These verses are from the New Revised Standard Version of the Bible, Catholic Edition; you may find other translations (such as the New American Bible, Revised Edition) more to your liking.

"The Lord, the Lord, a God merciful and gracious, slow to anger, and abounding in steadfast love and faithfulness." (Exodus 34:6)

"When I am afraid, I put my trust in you." (Psalm 56:3)

"Make a joyful noise to the Lord, all the earth. . . ." (Psalm 100)

"This is the day that the Lord has made; let us be glad and rejoice in it." (Psalm 118:24)

"O give thanks to the Lord, for he is good, for his steadfast love endures forever." (Psalm 136:1)

"I give you thanks, O Lord, with my whole heart." (Psalm 138:1)

"I praise you, for I am fearfully and wonderfully made." (Psalm 139:14)

"Let everything that breathes praise the Lord!" (Psalm 150:6)

"Bless the Lord, all you works of the Lord. . . ." (Daniel 3:26–45, Canticle of the Three Youths)

"I believe; help my unbelief." (Mark 9:24)

"Here am I, the servant of the Lord; let it be with me according to your word." (Luke 1:38)

"My soul magnifies the Lord. . . ."
(Luke 1:46–55, Canticle of Mary)

"Blessed be the Lord God of Israel. . . ."
(Luke 1:68–79, Canticle of Zechariah)

"Master, now you are dismissing your servant in peace. . . ." (Luke 2:29–32, Canticle of Simeon)

"God, be merciful to me, a sinner." (Luke 18:13)

"Jesus, remember me when you come into your kingdom." (Luke 23:42)

"Father, into your hands I commit My spirit."
(Luke 23:46)

"I can do all things through him who strengthens me." (Philippians 4:13)

Bless One Another

Come up with a short ritual for blessing your children during transitional times of the day (leaving or returning home, going to bed or waking, before a big event, etc.).
Here's how:

Make the Sign of the Cross on your child's forehead

while saying: "May God bless you and keep you, in the name of the Father, and of the Son, and of the Holy Spirit. Amen."

Seal the blessing with a kiss on the forehead.

Use **Holy Water** if you have it available.

Allow and encourage your kids to bless you as well.

You can find many more blessings in *Catholic Household Blessings and Prayers* (USCCB Publishing, 2007).

Learn More
CCC, 1669, 1671

Bless Your Home

You can bless your home using one of the many blessings and prayers for homes and households contained in *Catholic Household Blessings and Prayers*, including "Prayer Before Moving From a Home," "Blessing When Moving Into a New Home," "Blessing of the Home and Household on the Epiphany" (corresponding to the visit of the Magi to the Holy Family) and "Blessing of Homes During Eastertime" (a traditional time for the blessing of homes).

Better yet, invite your parish priest over for dinner and ask him to bless your home at the same time.

Talking Points: Why Bless Your Home?

Catholics bless their homes because God comes to meet them there. In its official blessings for homes, the Church recalls that Jesus spent much of his ministry sharing a meal with people in their homes: Zacchaeus the tax collector, Martha and Mary, and the disciples on the way to Emmaus, for example.

Christ continues to meet his people where they live; as a result, "every dwelling is a temple of holiness" ("Blessing of Homes During Eastertime," *Catholic Household Blessings and Prayers*, p. 129). It makes sense, then, that Catholics have long blessed their homes and households, asking God to protect them and make them places of peace and holiness.

Learn More

CCC, 1669, 1671

Celebrate the Anointing of the Sick

If a family member is seriously ill, frail, struggling with a chronic illness, about to undergo an operation, or in danger of death, ask your pastor (or another priest) to celebrate the sacrament of the Anointing of the Sick with them, being sure to include your children in the liturgy.

Whenever a family member has a more run-of-the-mill illness, be sure to have the family pray for them; see **Pray for the Sick** for ideas.

Talking Points: What is the Sacrament of Anointing?

The Sacrament of Anointing is one of the sacraments of healing. Once popularly known as "Last Rites," the Sacrament of Anointing is rooted in Jesus' charge to his apostles to anoint the sick with oil (Mark 6:13) as well as the practice of the early Church: "Are any among you sick? They should call for the elders of the church and have them pray over them, anointing them with oil in the name of the Lord. The prayer of faith will save the sick, and the Lord will raise them up; and anyone who has committed sins will be forgiven" (James 6:14-15). Because the priest acts "in the person of Christ" when administering the sacrament, those receiving the Sacrament of Anointing experience the healing touch of Jesus Christ.

Learn More
CCC, 1499–1532
Mark 6:13; James 5:14–15

Celebrate the Eucharist

The Eucharistic liturgy (the Mass) is the height of Christian prayer, and so essential to Christian life that the Church requires all the faithful to attend Mass every Sunday, as well as on holy days of obligation.

But many families find Mass challenging for one reason or another: disruptive children, resistant teenagers, apathy, or boredom. Below, you'll find some ideas for dealing with those challenges and making the most of your time at Mass.

General Suggestions

Educate your kids about the Eucharistic liturgy. Mass is an amazing experience: God speaks to us, we are transported to Calvary, we are physically and spiritually united with Christ, we are transformed and sent out on mission. Christ is at the heart of the Eucharistic celebration; the *Baltimore Catechism* summarizes this truth nicely: "The Holy Eucharist is a sacrament and a sacrifice. In the Holy Eucharist, under the appearances of bread and wine, the Lord Christ is contained, offered, and received." But it's difficult to appreciate what you don't understand. Fortunately, there is a wide variety of age-appropriate resources available to educate your kids about the significance of the Mass. You can find suggestions at pbgrace.com (look for this article).

Read and discuss the Scripture readings in advance. With older children and teens (or just with your spouse), read and reflect on the Scripture readings in advance (the day before Mass, for instance). Note that, except during special liturgical feasts and seasons, the readings from the Old Testament and the Gospel will share a common theme; you can begin your reflection by looking for what that theme is. You can also ask family members to comment on the readings: What was interesting? Surprising? Challenging? Enrich your understanding of the readings by using a missal with a commentary, by looking at the notes in your Bible, or finding a commentary online.

Make a point to offer thanks. The word *Eucharist* comes from Greek words that refer to giving thanks. That's what the first Christians, drawing on their Jewish heritage, would have done at mealtimes. They would offer prayers of blessing and thanksgiving not only for the food they were about to eat, but for all of God's work of creation, redemption, and sanctification (see *Catechism*, 1328). You can bring out this dimension of the Mass by asking your kids to name what they are thankful for on the way to church. Or have them write down what they are thankful for on slips of paper and place them in the collection basket during the offering of the gifts.

Do a liturgical scavenger hunt. Ask your kids to pay attention to certain elements of the Mass: the color of the vestments, the name of the books the Scripture readings are taken from, the order of the procession, the option used for the penitential rite, etc.

Walk to Mass. If you don't live close enough to walk, park a few blocks away and walk anyway. The transition may help older kids to get in the right mood—and younger kids might burn some energy.

Unpack the Mass. After Mass is over, talk about what you just experienced. If you didn't discuss the Scriptures in advance, discuss them on the way home, along with elements of the liturgy that seemed striking.

Younger Children

Sit up front. Sit as close to the front as possible, where children have the opportunity to observe the action of the Mass. Besides being more interesting than the view of someone else's back, having the opportunity to see what is going on week after week introduces children to the rhythm of the liturgy.

However, if you are mortally embarrassed by the behavior of your children, sitting in the back of the church is better than not attending Mass at all.

Explain what is going on. Before Mass, point out different features of the church—statues, stained glass windows, decorations, the tabernacle—and explain what they are about. During Mass, quietly point out key moments: "Now we're going to hear God speak to us." "We're kneeling because Jesus is here in a special way." Alternatively, redirect a disruptive child by asking her to (quietly) describe what she sees happening.

Invite participation. Children aged three and up can be invited to sing along with the basic responses, such as the Alleluia and Great Amen. Encourage them to genuflect towards the tabernacle as you enter and leave the church, and to kneel and stand appropriately during Mass.

Give them something appropriate to look at. Give young children a religious picture book or **Holy Card Key Chain**, or a favorite stuffed animal. (The animal can be encouraged to participate in Mass, too.)

Consequences. Promise a small reward for children who meet certain minimum standards of behavior (for example, not having to be removed). This method will only be effective if you are willing to follow through, however, so don't offer something you are unwilling to deny later, if necessary.

Introduce your child to the priest, lectors, musicians, and servers. If your parish sponsors a social hour after Mass, be sure your children get to know the priest and liturgical ministers. Recognizing these people as they celebrate the Mass will increase their engagement.

Play Mass at home. Prepare children to participate in the Mass by encouraging them to play Mass at home. You can purchase a play Mass kit from a Catholic store, or use materials around the house.

Don't be afraid to use the nursery or cry room. If your parish offers child care or a cry room, take advantage of it if it will help you participate in the Mass. Starting when little ones are around age three or four, try to keep your children in Mass so they can begin learning how to participate.

Should disruptive kids stay or go? Judging whether to remove a disruptive child is a balancing act. On the one hand, both you and your child are entitled to participate in the Mass by virtue of your baptism. On the other hand, so are other people! So the question often becomes: Is my child preventing other people from participating in the liturgy? The culture of the parish often determines where that line is drawn. If you are unsure, ask the pastor or a member of the parish.

Pray for help, and don't expect perfection. Hundreds of generations of moms and dads have experienced the same challenges as you; most of them are probably saints now, so you may as well ask them to pray for the strength and patience you need to get through Mass with small children. Remember, too, that the very work of lovingly managing children at Mass is a sort of prayer in itself.

Older Children

In addition to the ideas listed above, you can try the following ideas with children who have received their First Communion:

Give them a children's missal. Once children can read, give them a children's missal to help them follow along and participate during the Mass. There are a number of children's Mass books, or you can purchase a subscription to *MagnifiKid!*, a full-color subscription missal for children (magnificat.net/magnifikid).

Give them a children's prayer book. Children often have a hard time focusing on prayer after communion; help them out by providing them with a children's prayer book. See **Make a Prayer Book**.

Encourage children to serve in appropriate liturgical ministries. If your children are old enough, encourage them to become altar servers, to participate in the children's choir, to bring the gifts forward, or to serve as an usher or hospitality minister (with you). Directly participating in these ministries will give them a different perspective on the Mass and a sense of ownership.

Provide bonus points for participation. Offer some small reward for children who participate with appropriate posture, responses, singing, and so on.

Walk through the Mass. Set aside some time to walk your children through a different part of the Mass each week. Have them act it out, then explain the meaning of that part of the liturgy. Explore the symbolism of the actions and elements of the Mass: Why do we stand and kneel? (See **Kneel in Prayer**.) Why does the priest break the Eucharistic host? (It reflects the sharing action of Jesus at the Last Supper and the breaking of his body on the cross.) Why are bread and wine used? (See *CCC*, 1333–1336.)

Check out Scriptural connections. Nearly everything that the priest and the assembly say during the Mass is rooted in an ancient liturgical tradition. You can help your kids appreciate this long tradition by pointing out the many connections between the liturgy and the Scriptures. For example, the words, "Blessed are you, Lord God of all creation," spoken by the priest at the beginning of the Preparation of the Gifts, is an ancient Jewish prayer found in many biblical texts, including Luke 1:68 and Psalms 119:10; the Gloria (the sung acclamation that begins, "Glory to God in the highest. . .") is rooted in Luke 2:14 and Revelation 4:11, among others; and the priest's greeting ("The Lord be with you") and the people's response ("And with your Spirit") comes from 2 Timothy 4:22. Go to pbgrace. com for links to more examples.

Teens

Introduce a more mature understanding of the Mass. If the last time your teen learned about the Eucharist was while preparing for First Communion, it might be time for an update. Use a youth-friendly catechism or any of the many teen-friendly resources available online. LifeTeen.com offers excellent resources developed by teens and young adults; see pbgrace. com for other recommendations. Alternatively, academically gifted teens may want to dig into Church documents about the liturgy, such as the General Instruction of the Roman Missal.

Encourage service in appropriate liturgical ministries. Besides serving in the liturgical ministries listed above, teens who have been confirmed may also be eligible to become lectors or extraordinary ministers of the Eucharist.

Provide a missal. Offer your teen a missal to help him follow along during Mass.

Attend a teen-friendly parish. While "parish shopping" isn't ideal, if your child's faith is at stake, it might make sense to seek out a parish with a good youth program and a more teen-friendly liturgy—although some teens might find that a more traditional "smells and bells" liturgy provides a better environment for encountering Christ.

Should teens be forced to go to Mass? At the time of their marriage and at the baptism of their children, spouses promise to take responsibility for raising their children in the faith. Generally, this means insisting that children take part in the life of the Church. One way of thinking about this is safeguarding your child's spiritual welfare, much as you would safeguard his basic health and hygiene. However, resistance or rebelliousness around Mass attendance might signal other issues that need to be addressed (such as the parent-teen relationship or a need for deeper faith formation). Teens who insist that they no longer believe might be precluded from receiving the Eucharist on the grounds of being in a state of grave sin (*CCC*, 1395, 1415). If a teen is persistent in rejecting the faith, consideration also needs to be given to respect for his religious liberty (see Code of Canon Law, 748, §2). Seek the advice of your pastor for help in sorting out these difficult issues.

Talking Points: Why Do We Go to Mass?

The celebration of the Eucharist is so essential to Christian life that the Church requires all the faithful to attend Mass every Sunday, as well as on holy days of obligation, and to receive the Eucharist at least during the fifty days of the Easter season.

If your younger children ask why they "have to" attend Mass, explain to them that Mass is where we go to see and hear Jesus: "Jesus was born as a little baby because he wanted to be with us and share his love with us. After he went to be in heaven, he wanted to be even closer to us—all of us, all around the world—so he gave us some special ways of being close to him."

You can also adapt the answers below (which are more appropriate for older children and teens) to their level of understanding:

Because Jesus gave us himself in the Eucharist. "I am the living bread that came down from heaven; if any one eats of this bread, he will live forever; . . . he who eats my flesh and drinks my blood has eternal life and . . . abides in me, and I in him" (John 6:51, 54, 56). God chose to meet us by taking on flesh in Jesus Christ, and he chooses to continue meeting us "in the flesh" through the Eucharist, which is his whole body and blood, soul and divinity (*CCC,* 1413). We also encounter the presence of Christ during Mass in his Word (the Scriptures), the priest (who acts in the person of Christ), and the assembly of the faithful (*CCC,* 1088).

The Eucharist is at the heart of the life of the Church. Through the celebration of the Eucharist, Jesus' followers participate in the saving work of his life, death, and Resurrection (*CCC,* 1407, 1409), and prepare to continue that work in the world. The Eucharist also strengthens the unity of the Church as the Mystical Body of Christ (*CCC,* 1416).

The Eucharistic celebration is a sharing in heaven. When we go to Mass, we don't just anticipate heaven, we get to share in it (CCC, 1419).

Learn More
CCC, 1322–1419

Celebrate Reconciliation

Quick—what words come to mind when you think of going to confession? How about *conversion, healing, forgiveness, reconciliation, honesty, courage,* or even *celebration*?

The Church uses all of those words to describe the sacrament of penance and reconciliation. It is one of the two sacraments of *healing* (the other being the anointing of the sick); it is sometimes called the sacrament of *conversion*, the sacrament of *confession*, or the sacrament of *forgiveness*. Pope John Paul II called it an act of *honesty and courage*. And the *Catechism* refers to it as a *celebration* eight times.

All of those descriptions belie the popular stereotype of the sacrament of penance and reconciliation as focusing primarily on guilt. In fact, many who attend the sacrament use another word to describe its effects: *joy*.

If you haven't been to the sacrament of penance and reconciliation as a family, give it a try. Better yet, try making it a habit. Like any healthy practice (think of exercise or flossing), getting started might be a challenge, but if you stick with it, you'll be pleasantly surprised by the results. Here are some tips:

Identify obstacles. If your family doesn't regularly participate in the sacrament of reconciliation, think about why that is. Maybe you or other family members have objections to going (check out the list of common objections, below). Or maybe the reason is more practical. If so, read on for some strategies.

Model reconciliation. Practice reconciliation at home. Show your children what it looks like by apologizing to your spouse (or other adults) for small transgressions. More powerfully, apologize to your children: "I wish I hadn't done that to you; I'm sorry I did." Keep it simple and straightforward, and show that admitting fault is not a sign of weakness, but strength.

Coach reconciliation. Kids of all ages (and not a few adults) often have difficulty moving through a conflict to reconciliation. You can help them out by coaching them through it. Have them sit down in chairs and work through the conflict as much as they can themselves, providing help or advice as needed. (A five-minute silent cooling off period might help.) Teach them how to voice their grievances in a way that sticks to the facts and respects the other person's dignity; teach them how to listen and respond constructively; and teach them how to apologize. These are difficult skills, even for adults; see pbgrace.com for links to helpful resources.

Understand the sacrament. Many Catholics have misconceptions about the sacrament of penance and reconciliation. If you or your older children or teens haven't learned anything new about the sacrament since the second grade, investigate a more mature understanding of the sacrament.

Find a time that works. Find confession times at local parishes and go to the one that best fits your schedule; sometimes parishes even offer confession during weekdays. If you can't find a time that works, schedule a special appointment with your pastor. He might even be willing to offer the sacrament before or after Sunday Mass.

Develop a habit. Make regular confession a habit by scheduling it on your calendar and giving it the same priority as a dentist or car maintenance appointment. Start by committing to attend three times a year: once during Advent, once during Lent, and once over the summer. If you already go that often, make it a habit to go once a month.

Young children? Go early. If you are attending confession with young children or babies, show up ten minutes early to be near the front of the line; if you are lucky, the priest may show up early, too.

Help kids overcome nervousness. Kids are often nervous the first few times they participate in the sacrament of penance and reconciliation. Help them out by providing them with an

Examination of Conscience. Provide them with a written Act of Contrition (the prayer that the penitent prays during the sacrament). Reassure them that the priest will help them out. And finally, attend with them; go first so they can see you emerge unscathed!

Practice a Daily Examen. Incorporate the **Daily Examen** into your routine in the days leading up to the sacrament, as a way of raising your children's awareness of where they need healing and forgiveness.

Talking Points: Overcoming Objections

Most Catholics do not participate in the sacrament of penance and reconciliation for one reason or another. Here are some common objections that might be raised by your kids, and some responses you might try out:

I don't know what to confess. If your kids don't know what to confess, help them out by doing a **Daily Examen** for several days before confession; then, provide them with a printed **Examination of Conscience** (available from many websites online, or see the sample examination of conscience for children in **A Handful of Catholic Prayers**).

I haven't done anything bad enough to confess. Encourage kids—especially older children and teens—to think not only about what they did wrong, but how they have fallen short of being the person God made them to be. Even saints, priests, and religious sisters and brothers regularly celebrate the sacrament of penance and reconciliation, recognizing that the grace of the sacrament strengthens them to follow God's will more perfectly, and so become more truly themselves. Comparing the person we have been to the saint we would like to be opens up all sorts of possibilities for confession.

Confession is all about guilt and shame; I believe in a loving God. The reality of God's unconditional love lies at the heart of the sacrament, which recalls the parable of the Prodigal Son

(*CCC*, 1439, 1465). Because God loves us, he wants to heal us of whatever hurts us—most especially sin. We don't go to confession in order to focus on what bad people we are; we go to confession because ignoring our sins doesn't make them go away. Just as we bring our physical injuries to the doctor for healing, we go to confession to be healed of our sins (*CCC*, 1456).

I am too embarrassed or ashamed. It is natural for children to feel shy about confessing their sins in front of a priest. Simple repetition is the best remedy to this issue, although depending on the child, it might help to get to know the priest better outside of confession—or to confess with a different priest at another parish. It might help to remind your child that, during the sacrament, the priest acts in the person of Christ; it is Jesus who hears and forgives our sins. Read stories of Jesus' mercy toward sinners to reinforce the point. Finally, remind your child that anything he or she confesses must be kept secret by the priest (*CCC*, 1467).

Why can't I just ask God for forgiveness directly? Anyone can pray to God for forgiveness at any time, as King David did (see Psalm 51 for a beautiful song of repentance). However, God came to us in Jesus in order to forgive us "in the flesh," and he continues to do so even today by making the whole Church the sign and instrument of his forgiveness. In the sacrament of penance and reconciliation, then, the priest, acting in the person of Christ, makes the tender mercy of God tangible. Moreover, Catholics confess their sins before a priest in recognition that their sins not only hurt their relationship with God, but one another, and especially the Church (*CCC*, 1441–1445).

Learn More
Matthew 16:19; John 20:23
CCC, 1422–1498

Consecrate Your Family

Consider consecrating your family to the Holy Family.

To consecrate something means to associate it with something sacred. By formally associating your family with Jesus, Mary, and Joseph, you ask for their care and for the grace to model your own family after theirs.

The Apostolate for Family Consecration offers a wealth of resources for family consecration at Familyland.org. See pb-grace.org for links to other resources.

Contemplative Prayer

Contemplative prayer is one of the three "expressions of prayer" described by the *Catechism* (the others are **Vocal Prayer** and **Meditative Prayer**). Contemplative prayer is a simple resting in the love of Christ. Rather than taking the initiative (as with vocal prayer and meditation), contemplative prayer is about silencing ourselves so God can work in us. St. Thérèse of Lisieux described contemplative prayer as a close sharing between friends, while St. John Vianney described it as gazing at Christ and allowing Christ to gaze at us.

Contemplation may not seem suited to wiggly, squirmy, eye-rolling, "Are-we-done-yet?" kids. But this intimate basking in Christ's love is something kids deserve to know about. And you never know when your kids might surprise you. Many religious educators successfully teach contemplative and meditative prayer to children on a regular basis. The Catholic Diocese of Townsville, Australia, offers a comprehensive website on teaching meditation and contemplation to children at cominghome.org.au.

Young Children

With younger kids, focus on modeling prayerful silence: "Mom and Dad are going to be quiet to listen to God now. You be quiet, too, and listen to what God (or Jesus, or the angels) might be saying to you." Then close your eyes and really pray quietly for a few minutes. Ignore their chatter and noise (it might help to strap them into a high chair first!). Your goal with young children is to simply model this form of prayer. With enough repetition, even very young children will eventually begin to imitate your example. In the meantime, this moment of silent resting in God's presence might just become a refreshing "reset button" that makes it easier to deal with your kids patiently.

Older Children and Teens

With older children, try contemplation for increasingly longer periods of time: three minutes, then five, then ten, and fifteen minutes or longer for kids who have more training with this spiritual exercise. When first beginning this practice, their goal might be to simply maintain an attitude of quiet alertness.

Here is one way to teach older children and teens contemplative prayer

1. Prepare. If you are able, create a prayerful environment by lighting a candle or striking a bell (see **Smells and Bells**).

2. Listening to "sheer silence." Explain to your children that contemplative prayer is all about creating a space inside of ourselves to meet the loving presence of Jesus. This involves a quieting of our minds and an alert attentiveness to God's presence. As an example, you might read the Bible passage about the prophet Elijah waiting for the presence of the Lord (1 Kings 19:11–13). Elijah is told to come out of his cave, because the Lord will be passing by. First he witnesses a great wind, then an earthquake, and then a fire; but Elijah does not find the presence of the Lord in any of those things. It is only when he hears "a sound of sheer silence" that Elijah comes out of his cave to stand before the presence of the Lord.

3. Enter contemplation via meditation. Even people who have long experience with contemplative prayer rarely enter directly into it; it's not like flipping a light switch. Many people find it helpful to enter contemplation via meditation. For instance, your children might choose a sentence or phrase to occasionally repeat interiorly to help them focus on Jesus, or to call on the assistance of the Holy Spirit. Another technique involves focusing on a mental picture of Jesus in a peaceful setting. See **Meditative Prayer** for more ideas.

4. Let go of outcomes. As much as possible, spend the time praying rather than monitoring your kids' prayerfulness . . . and don't worry too much about results. Focus on simply introducing them to this spiritual exercise; the invitation to contemplative prayer may be one they respond to at a time of conversion or crisis later in life.

Besides trying this type of prayer during your **Family Prayer Time**, you can suggest that older children practice contemplative prayer after receiving the Eucharist, during Eucharistic Adoration, or before falling asleep.

Learn More
CCC, 2709–2719

Daily Examen

A Daily Examen (or an Examen of Consciousness) is a prayerful method of "checking in" on how well we are living out our Christian faith on a daily basis. Developed by St. Ignatius of Loyola more than four hundred years ago, the Examen invites us to reflect on how God has been present in our day, how we have responded to that presence, and how we might grow in holiness. Note that the Examen is different from an **Examination of Conscience**, the practice of reviewing the health of your spiritual life before receiving the sacrament of Penance and Reconciliation.

If you make the Examen a regular part of your family prayer, you may want to encourage older children and teens to write down their responses to the various prompts in a Prayer Journal.

Younger Children

Introduce very young children to the idea of reviewing the day and bringing it to God by doing **Highs and Lows**. For children ages five through nine, try talking through the steps conversationally, using this shortened method:

1. Enter God's presence. Set a prayerful tone (see **Smells and Bells** for some ideas). Say: "Let's pray about our day." Make the Sign of the Cross. "God, you have been with us all day long, since the time we woke up until now; help us to remember our day, so we can bring it to you."

2. What happened today? Review the events of the day, moving through the parts of the day and offering prompts as necessary. "What happened in the morning when we woke up? . . . What happened at school? . . . When we got home? . . . When were we angry? . . . Sad? . . . Happy? . . . What was beautiful? . . . What was amazing?" Optionally, write down responses on a dry erase board or in a prayer journal.

3. How was God present, and how did we respond? "How was God present to us today?" You will probably need to name this for your children at first, or supplement their responses with your own suggestions. It might be obvious that God is present in moments of beauty and joy, but you can help your children see how God is also present during times of challenge and sadness. Ask, "How did we respond to God's presence? When were we loving? When weren't we loving?"

4. Pray the day. Invite your children to think about what Jesus is saying to them through the events of the day. Ask guiding questions such as, "What do you think Jesus says about our day?" Invite them to pray in response: "What do we want to tell Jesus about what happened today?" Encourage simple words of praise, thankfulness, repentance, forgiveness, and petitions for the grace to draw closer to God in the coming day. Close with the Sign of the Cross.

Older Children and Teens

Try the traditional form of the Examen during **Family Prayer Time** with older children and teens, setting aside ten to fifteen minutes to do it well. What follows is a simple outline; you can find more detailed versions, as well as more background information, at IgnatianSpirituality.com or at pbgrace.com.

Consider lighting a candle or playing quiet music to set a prayerful atmosphere. Briefly describe each step, allowing several minutes for each one.

1. Enter God's presence. Take a few moments to quiet down, to recall that God has accompanied you every step of the way during the day, and to open yourself to God's presence.

2. Review the events of the day in a spirit of gratitude. Move through your day, hour by hour, taking special note of its many small gifts: the warmth of a child's hand, a cup of coffee, a flock of birds, the kindness of a stranger. Recall that God is revealed in each of these details. Think, too, about the gifts you were able to give others: an encouraging word, a smile, work well done.

3. Pray for the "Spirit of truth." Prepare for the next step by asking for the "Spirit of truth" to "guide you into all truth" (John 16:13). Prepare yourself to be honest as you examine your actions during the day, knowing that the truth will free you to grow closer to God. Recall, too, God's unconditional love for you.

4. How were you open to God's presence in the events of the day? Next, examine how you responded (or didn't) to God's presence in the key events of the day. When were you loving? When did you miss an opportunity to love? When were you sinful? How much were you in charge of your actions, and what did you do out of simple habit? Pay attention to your emotions around these events. St. Ignatius taught that the Holy Spirit often speaks to us through our emotions, even the "negative" ones. What truth might God be revealing to you through your emotions?

5. Bring it to Jesus. Finally, respond in prayer to the insights revealed in the previous steps. You may want to imagine this as a friendly face-to-face meeting with Jesus, one in which you offer words of sorrow, gratitude, or joy. You may want to ask for forgiveness, consolation, encouragement, the grace to overcome bad habits, and direction for how to grow closer to God. Close with the Sign of the Cross, and continue to listen to Jesus throughout the rest of your day.

Dance Your Prayer

David danced before the ark of the Lord "with all his might" (2 Samuel 6:14), the Psalms exhort us to praise the Lord with dancing (Psalm 149:3; Psalm 150:4), and in the Parable of the

Prodigal Son, the return of the prodigal son is greeted with music and dancing (Luke 15:25).

Although the Church does not allow dance in the public liturgy of Western cultures, dance has a long tradition as a joyful response to God's love, and the Church recognizes it as a form of popular piety. Children are especially receptive to dancing their prayer. To try it, follow these tips:

Find some danceable Christian music. SpiritandSong.com features plenty of contemporary Catholic music, both liturgical and popular, including free downloads. Seeds Family Worship (seedsfamilyworship.net) offers danceable music with lyrics taken directly from Scripture. You can find more possibilities at pbgrace.com, or search the Internet for "Christian children's music."

Set expectations in advance. Tell your kids in advance how long you'll be dancing for, in terms of minutes or number of songs. Set ground rules as necessary ("No dancing on the table!").

Save dancing for special occasions. Gaudete Sunday, Laetare Sunday, Easter, or other joyful feasts and observances (such as a child's baptismal anniversary) might be a good time for a little dancing prayer.

Provide some context. Talk about why it's an appropriate time for such joyful prayer, briefly explaining the occasion for the celebration.

Learn More
CCC, 1674

Discernment

As teens grow older, they begin to make important life choices for themselves: vocation, career, post-secondary schooling, volunteer opportunities, and relationships, to name a few. You can help them face these decisions by introducing them to the spiritual practice of discernment.

Discernment involves perceiving which of two or more seemingly good or neutral choices best conforms to God's will. Should you pursue a career in nursing or music? Should you continue in a romantic relationship, or is it time to break it off? Should you enter religious life, or are you called to married life?

Christians don't bear the burden of making these decisions alone. Instead, they strive to discern the best course by turning to God in prayer, then carefully attending to God's response. The process of discernment, which may take some time to unfold, usually draws on rational analysis (such as listing pros and cons), critical examination of emotions and feelings (how do these options make me feel, and why?), and consideration of the wisdom and advice of others.

Over the centuries, saints and mystics have developed many methods of discernment that Catholics still draw on today. A full introduction to these methods is beyond the scope of this book, but links to resources on spiritual discernment can be found at pbgrace.com.

Eucharistic Adoration

Eucharistic Adoration is the practice of praying before Jesus in the form of the Eucharistic host. The host may be exposed in a special vessel known as a monstrance, or reserved in a tabernacle. (The tabernacle is the place where the Eucharistic hosts are kept after the celebration of Mass; it is indicated by a light or candle.)

Many larger Catholic communities sponsor perpetual (around-the-clock) adoration before the exposed Eucharist in a special chapel that is open to the public. Sometimes parishes will hold a more limited time of Eucharistic Adoration (such as the Forty Hours Devotion), especially during holy seasons.

Where perpetual Eucharistic Adoration is available, individuals are invited to sign up for a regular hour. However, adoration is also open to anyone who wants to come and spend time in the presence of the Blessed Sacrament.

People pray in all sorts of ways during Eucharistic Adoration. **Meditative Prayer**, **Contemplative Prayer**, and silent conversation with Jesus are common practices, as is saying the rosary (see **Pray the Rosary**). Some people sing hymns of praise (if they are alone), while others write in a prayer journal or bring sacred reading. But Eucharistic Adoration can also be as simple as sunbathing . . . just sitting and soaking up God's love in the presence of Jesus.

Younger Children
Recalling Jesus' command to "let the little children come to me" (Matthew 19:14), many Catholic parents bring even very young children, including infants and toddlers, to Eucharistic

Adoration. Because young children may be distracting to other people, however, check with your pastor or the person responsible for organizing adoration hours to see whether the practice is generally accepted in your parish.

Avoid bringing food or noisy toys into the adoration chapel; however, you might bring religious picture books, a **Holy Card Key Chain**, or crayons and religious coloring sheets. If you are lucky enough to have the chapel to yourselves, you can lead your children in a modified version of the rosary (see **Pray the Rosary**) or in singing religious songs.

Older Children and Teens

Pope Benedict XVI recommended that children be taught to appreciate spending time in the presence of the Eucharist as part of their preparation for First Communion (*Sacramentum Caritatis*, 67). Here are some tips for introducing children to this practice:

Teach your children about the real presence of Christ in the Eucharist. See the *Talking Points* under **Celebrate the Eucharist** or CCC, 1373–1381.

Take your children to Mass regularly. The celebration of the Eucharistic liturgy is the "source and summit of Christian life" (CCC, 1324); Eucharistic Adoration flows from the Mass. See **Celebrate the Eucharist**.

Practice reverence for the Eucharist. Genuflect and make the Sign of the Cross before the tabernacle in church, and say a prayer when you pass a Catholic church.

Keep it short. Keep your first visits to the Blessed Sacrament short—say, ten minutes. If Eucharistic adoration becomes a regular practice for your family, you can gradually increase the time.

Offer aids to prayer. Give your children a rosary, children's prayer book, or a journal for writing down their prayers to Jesus.

Teach children that reverence for the Eucharist doesn't end in the adoration chapel. The Eucharist incorporates us into the Body of Christ and strengthens us to continue Jesus' mission in the world, especially among the poor (see CCC, 1397).

Talking Points: Why Eucharistic Adoration?

Children (and some adults) might wonder why Catholics practice devotion to the Eucharist; after all, isn't God present always and everywhere?

While it is true that we can pray to God anywhere, the Eucharist holds a privileged place in Christian worship because in it, Christ is fully present: body and blood, soul and divinity (see CCC, 1374). Think of it this way: In his love, God wants to be as close to us as possible; this is why he became incarnate—flesh and blood—in Jesus. But even as he was preparing to leave us in that form, he wanted to continue to remain physically, intimately present with us, so he gave us the Eucharist (see CCC, 1380). And it is through the Eucharist that we become the Body of Christ, the Church, thus continuing his physical presence and his mission in the world.

Learn More
CCC, 1378–1379, 1418

Examination of Conscience

Before you celebrate the sacrament of penance and reconciliation with your kids (see **Celebrate Reconciliation**), help them to prepare by coaching them through an examination of conscience.

An examination of conscience is a prayerful reflection on our actions in light of our faith in order to identify sins, patterns of sin, or ways that we are falling short of who God is calling us to be. Once we recognize our sins, we can ask God for forgiveness and healing. (For more *Talking Points* about this topic, see **Celebrate Reconciliation**.)

A good examination of conscience considers all areas of our lives—our thoughts and words, what we have done, and what we have failed to do (to paraphrase the Confiteor). Typically it consists of questions in three categories: the call to love God, the call to love others, and the call to love one's self. Most forms of the examination of conscience draw on the Ten Commandments; however, some draw on the Beatitudes, Catholic social teaching, or portions of the *Catechism*.

You can find many forms of the examination of conscience in various prayer books and online; the U.S. Catholic bishops provide versions that use the Ten Commandments and the principles of Catholic social teaching, as well as versions geared toward children, young adults, single adults, and married adults on their website (search the Internet for the terms *USCCB* and *examination of conscience*). A simple examination of conscience for children is also included in **A Handful of Catholic Prayers** at the back of this book.

Here are some tips for making a good examination of conscience:

Ask for help. Encourage your kids to pray to the Holy Spirit to enlighten them about their sins, or ways that they have fallen short of being the person God is calling them to be.

Don't wait until the last minute. If you use a written examination of conscience as a guide, post it on your refrigerator or in your **Home Oratory** a few days before going to receive the sacrament of penance and reconciliation.

Pray the Examen. Praying the Ignatian Examen regularly as a family will help older kids and teens become more aware of their spiritual lives generally, and make their examinations of conscience more fruitful.

Learn More
CCC, 1454

Fasting

Fasting and abstinence are the practice of giving up something good (for example, food or meat) in order to turn away from sin and draw closer to God. It is not only a form of penance, but a spiritual discipline that helps us make room for God, strengthens our will, prepares us for mission, and puts us in solidarity with the suffering of Christ and suffering people around the world.

Besides observing the formal requirements for fasting and abstinence laid out by the Church, most Catholics traditionally choose additional penitential practices during Lent. Beginning at about age five or six, children can be encouraged to "give something up," or to adopt a positive practice, as a way of entering into the spirit of Lent.

This type of fasting doesn't need to be limited to the forty days of Lent, though. Your family may want to fast for a few days as a form of intense prayer for a special intention, such as a loved one who is gravely ill, or a crisis in the news.

Older Kids and Teens

When encouraging your kids to fast, help them brainstorm some creative ideas. A positive experience is more likely if you make the fast concrete and measurable. For example, instead of just saying, "I'll stop fighting with my sister," sit down and figure out specific actions that will lead to a "conversion" in this area. What causes the fighting? If the problem is borrowing clothes without permission, make that part of the fast. A chart or special jar (with coins or marbles to mark achievement) might also help your kids keep on track.

Here are some ideas for things your kids can give up or take on for Lent:

Give up the usual suspects. Sweets, video games, soda, junk food, social media, and other creature comforts.

Quiet it down. Monks practice silence in order to better hear God. Your family can, too, by turning off radios and music players (maybe just in the car), turning off the television, eating a meal in silence (or while listening to some sacred reading), practicing **Thirty Seconds of Silence**, being silent for the first fifteen minutes of the morning, or even having a day of silence.

Make your room or home a desert. Jesus spent forty days in the desert. Kids and teens can imitate his example by making their room more desert-like as well, removing pictures and posters from walls, putting away rugs and comforters, emptying closets and dressers of all but the most essential outfits, throwing extra clutter (gadgets, trinkets, toys) in a box to be stored away.

Slim down your wardrobe. Kids can count up the number of outfits they have and select ten percent to wear during their fast. (For inspiration, read the stories of saints who gave away their clothes to the poor.) At the end of the fast, they can consider donating some of the clothes they didn't wear.

Perform a random act of kindness every day. Perform a different random act of kindness every day; doing it secretly makes it more fun. See RandomActsOfKindness.org for ideas.

Write your fight. Older kids can cut down on sibling squabbling by committing to writing down their complaints rather than making them verbally. Print out "complaint forms" that include guidelines for rephrasing complaints using respectful language.

Pray it up. Teens and preteens can carry a rosary with them, using it to pray throughout the day. Any set of beads (such as a beaded necklace or bracelet) could be used to keep track of prayers.

Wear your faith. Kids can be encouraged to wear Christian symbols (a necklace, bracelet, or t-shirt) as a witness to their faith—and to remind them to live out their beliefs more consistently. See **Wear Your Prayer**.

Share. Older kids who are especially possessive of their toys or bedroom space can be encouraged to share, actively and kindly, with their siblings. Or encourage kids to share by donating the money they saved from their sacrifices (for example, giving up junk food) to a charitable cause.

Practice being present. Teens can commit to putting down their phone (or other electronic device) when someone is present with them. Even better: create phone-free zones (like the dinner table).

Get to know Jesus. Have kids read one of the Gospels in an age-appropriate Bible, or read it together as a family, over the course of Lent. The Gospel of Mark may be read in one long sitting.

Talking Points: Why Do We Fast?

Here are some ways Christians think about fasting:

As penance. Throughout the Old Testament, people covered themselves in ashes, took off their fine clothes, and fasted in order to express their repentance from sin. Fasting serves a similar purpose today.

Making room for God. By emptying ourselves, even if just a little bit, we make room for God to enter our lives more fully. When fasting and abstinence are hard, we are moved to turn to God in prayer for help.

Strengthening the will. Fasting is a spiritual discipline; just as physical exercise makes our body stronger, fasting strengthens our will. Practicing self-denial in small things strengthens our will to resist sin in other areas of our lives.

A preparation for mission. For Christians, fasting imitates the forty days that Jesus spent in the desert. Just as Jesus used this time to prepare for his public mission, fasting prepares us to continue his mission in the world.

Solidarity with the suffering Christ. Whatever small suffering we experience when we fast brings us closer to the suffering Christ—and all the people who suffer from hunger, malnutrition, and abuse on a daily basis.

Talking Points: When Do Catholics Fast and Abstain?

In the United States, the Church calls on Catholics ages eighteen through fifty-nine to the regular practice of fasting and abstinence from meat; pregnant and nursing mothers, as well as the sick, are exempted.

Fasting is defined as consuming only one full meal and, if necessary, two smaller meals (less than one full meal combined) throughout the day, with no snacks between meals. Abstinence means not eating meat, such as poultry, beef, and pork. Fish, meat-based broths, eggs, butter, and other animal-derived products are allowed.

Adults are required to fast on Ash Wednesday and Good

Friday, with the Good Friday fast ideally lasting through Saturday evening. In addition, everyone ages fourteen and older is required to abstain from meat on Ash Wednesday and the Fridays of Lent. Abstaining from meat is strongly encouraged on all Fridays throughout the year, but not required as long as some other penitential practice replaces it (for example, giving up sweets or performing some charitable work).

The United States Conference of Catholic Bishops posts information about fasting and abstinence requirements on the "Fasting and Abstinence" page of its website, usccb.org.

Learn More
Deuteronomy 9:9, 18, 25–29; 10:10; 1 Kings 19:7–18; Daniel 9:1–19; Jonah 3; Matthew 4:1–11
CCC, 1434, 1438, 2043

Highs and Lows

At the end of the day (perhaps over dinner), have each person share his or her "highs" and "lows" for the day: What was the best thing that happened today? What was the worst?

Explain that we can give the events of our days back to God in prayer. We can give the "highs" back to God in the form of our joy and thanks, and we can give the lows back to God by "offering them up"—that is, uniting our suffering (no matter how small) with the suffering of Christ on the cross, so that God might take our suffering and turn it into something good, just as he did in the Resurrection.

Say a simple prayer such as the Our Father or a spontaneous prayer of your own, or sing a simple song, as a way of offering your highs and lows to God.

For a more involved version of this practice, see **Daily Examen**.

Invocations

Invocations (or "pious invocations") are very short prayers—usually a phrase or sentence—that can be said once (as a quick, spontaneous prayer during stressful or busy times) or repeated over and over as a way of meditating on the presence of God.

Teach your kids these quick prayers, perhaps focusing on one a week. You can find extensive lists of invocations online or in *Catholic Household Blessings and Prayers*. Here are a few examples:

- "Father, into your hands I commend my spirit." (Luke 23:46)

- "Holy Mary, Mother of God, pray for us."

- "All you holy men and women, pray for us."

- "Holy Spirit, give me strength."

- "Save me, Lord!"

- "Jesus Christ, Son of God, have mercy on me, a sinner." (Luke 18:13)

- "My Lord and my God!" (John 20:28)

- "Jesus, Mary, and Joseph, I trust in you."

- "All for you, Lord."

- "I love you, Lord."

- "Teach me to give and not count the cost." (St. Ignatius of Loyola)

- "Lord, let me be what I should be." (St. Catherine of Sienna)

Kneel in Prayer

The next time you gather for **Family Prayer Time**, try kneeling as you pray. Genuflect (kneel on one knee) before the Blessed Sacrament as you enter and leave church.

Talking Points: Why Kneel?

Why do Catholics kneel during certain parts of the liturgy? Kneeling is a posture of reverence and prayer, especially supplication. In ancient times, it was common for subjects to kneel before their rulers as an expression of humility and respect. And because of the way kneeling makes a person vulnerable, it is also an expression of trust. Kneeling during prayer is an expression of humility and respect and trust toward God, our ultimate "ruler."

Although standing was the most common prayer posture among the ancient Israelites and for most Christians until the Middle Ages, there are also many early references to kneeling in prayer: "O come, let us worship and bow down, let us kneel before the LORD, our Maker!" (Psalm 95:6) The New Testament also makes many references to kneeling in prayer.

Finally, kneeling can help kids (and adults) focus on prayer;

it is another **Smells and Bells** way of opening ourselves to the presence of God.

Learn More
1 Kings 8:54; Matthew 2:11; 17:14; 20:20; Mark 1:40; 10:17; Luke 22:41; Acts 9:40; 20:36; 21:5; Romans 14:11; Philippians 2:10

Lectio Divina

Lectio divina or "sacred reading," is an ancient method of praying with sacred texts that dates to the fourth century. Usually the sacred text comes from the Scriptures, but other texts may be used as well, such as the writings of the saints. The basic idea is to spend time listening deeply and intently to what God might have to say to you through the text—almost as if the sacred text were a much-cherished love letter from God.

Lectio divina takes many forms, but traditionally it is divided into four steps: *lectio* (reading), *meditatio* (meditation), *oratio* (prayer), and *contemplatio* (contemplation). These steps do not necessarily need to be followed in a rigid order, although it may help to spend five minutes on reading, five on meditation, five on prayer, and five on contemplation. It is important, however, to touch on all four movements.

There are many books and online resources on *lectio divina* that you can use to explore this practice more deeply. One worth mentioning is *Lectio Divina for Children and Teens: Activities to Help Young People Encounter God's Word* by Jared Dees (TheReligionTeacher.com, 2013).

Lectio Made Super Simple

If the steps outlined below seem overwhelming, back up and begin by reading a short sacred text slowly, perhaps two or three times. Invite your kids to respond by offering a word, phrase, or image that especially caught their attention. Why did that part of the text stand out? Talk about how God speaks to us through our sacred texts. What might God be saying in the reading? How might you respond?

See **Sacred Story Time** for a guide to using lectio divina with young children.

Older Kids and Teens

1. Reading. First, select a short reading—the shorter, the better: a paragraph or two, or even a sentence or two. Traditionally, the text is taken from the Scriptures or the writings of the saints. The Gospel or Old Testament reading for the upcoming Sunday is an excellent choice for families just beginning to practice *lectio divina*. Read the text slowly and carefully. Explain words or situations your children may not understand, consulting footnotes or commentaries as necessary. Read the text slowly two or three times, allowing a brief pause between readings.

2. Meditation. Invite your kids to reflect on the meaning of the passage. You can offer guiding questions such as: What words or images stood out for you? Why? What does the reading mean to you? Does it say anything important about your life right now? Spend just a few minutes sharing as a family.

3. Prayer. Invite your kids to pray over the insights that arose for them during step 2 (meditation). This can be done silently or out loud; if your family is just beginning *lectio*, you may want to offer the prayer yourself on behalf of the whole family, in order to provide an example. During the prayer step, you might offer thanksgiving to God for important insights that emerged from the text. Or, if the text was difficult to meditate on, you might ask God for guidance and clarity. If the text was challenging or caused anxiety, you might ask God for humility, strength, and the ability to trust in providence.

4. Contemplation. The fourth step of *lectio divina* is sometimes called "resting in the Word of God." Invite your kids to still themselves and attend to God's presence. God may speak to them in a particular way, or may just be with them in silence. (See **Contemplative Prayer** for more about the practice of contemplation.)

5. Wrapping up. End with a blessing or the Sign of the Cross.

Learn More
CCC, 2708
General Directory for Catechesis, 71

Let Kids Lead

Giving kids leadership responsibility appropriate to their development can boost their interest and investment in your family's prayer life—and research shows that kids who have leadership responsibility for faith practices are more likely to continue them as adults.

Younger Children

Give choices. Let younger children choose which prayer to say; see **Grab-Bag Prayers** for some fun ways to do this.
Start prayer. Let them "lead" by saying the first few words of the prayer before everyone else joins in.

Let them pray for you. Invite them to pray for you—for example, to bless you at bedtime after you bless them, or to pray over you when you are sick or sad.

Older Children and Teens

Lead the rosary. Let older children and teens lead the rosary or other prayers, with help from you as necessary (see **Pray the Rosary**).

Prepare for prayer. Let them prepare part of your **Family Prayer Time**—the list of intentions, for example, or the choice of song.

Light a candle. Let them light the prayer candle or strike a bell to call you to prayer (see **Smells and Bells**).

Plan a prayer service. Invite teens to plan and lead a prayer service for **Family Prayer Time** that incorporates music, prayers, readings, and candles, incense, or bells. If they are especially ambitious, refer them to Church documents on liturgical practice, beginning with paragraphs 1136–1199 in the *Catechism* or its parallel in a teen catechism.

Serve the Church. Encourage older kids and teens to serve in liturgical ministries that are open to them: youth choir, altar server, usher, etc.

List Your Prayer Intentions

Keep a list of your family's ongoing prayer intentions on a piece of paper or a dedicated dry erase board. Post the list on your refrigerator, by the bathroom mirror, or in your **Home Oratory**. Invite family members to add to the list as they think of prayer intentions throughout the day.

Encourage people to say a prayer for an intention on the list throughout the day. Make the list of prayer intentions the focus of your family prayer time every few days by reading the list and then offering the intentions up to God with a simple prayer, a moment of silence, or a rosary.

Examples of intentions might include:

- sick friends or relatives;

- difficult situations at work or school;

- resolution of family problems (for example, better relations between siblings);

- issues of peace and justice in the news (such as for the resolution of armed conflict, help for victims of natural disaster, etc.);

- thanksgiving for answered prayers.

You can also find intentions for intercessory prayer in *Catholic Household Blessings and Prayers*.

Talking Points: The Universal Prayer
Prayers offered for the needs of others are known as inter-

cessory prayers, while prayers for our own needs are known as petitionary prayers. (See **Pray the Five Forms of Prayer**.) Praying intercessory prayers at home echoes the practice of the Church when, during the Mass, we offer the Universal Prayer (Prayer of the Faithful). You can remind your kids of the connection by using the same format that is typically used in Mass: a leader says, "For (intention), let us pray," and the rest of the people offer a common response such as, "Lord, hear our prayer."

Learn More
CCC, 2632–2636

Meditate on Sacred Art

The Church has long relied on art to proclaim the Gospel. This was especially true when most people were illiterate, but even today, sacred art expresses truth and wisdom that cannot be conveyed by words alone.

Use sacred art during **Family Prayer Time** as a way of practicing **Meditative Prayer**. You can find sacred art online (search for "sacred art" or "biblical art," or find links to index websites at pbgrace.com); in books (such as the many titles by Sister Wendy Beckett or the Illuminated Rosary series); or in a church or art museum. It might enrich your experience to research the artwork before you pray with it.

One kind of sacred art that is created for the specific purpose of meditative prayer is the icon. A particular tradition of the Eastern Orthodox Church, icons use highly symbolic "language" to engage the viewer in prayer. In fact, the artist (or ico-nographer) is said to "write" the icon, and the viewer is called to "read" the language of the icon with her heart. Icons usually depict some holy person—Jesus, Mary, or the saints—gazing directly at the viewer. It is through those gazing eyes that the viewer is intended to pass through the painting itself into a mystical encounter with God.

See below for one approach to prayerfully meditating on sacred art.

Younger Children

When you read religious picture books to younger children, be sure to linger with the pictures in order to help your children respond to the story. That response to God's word, as basic as it may be, is also a form of prayer. Ask guiding questions similar to those outlined above:

- What is happening in the picture? What details do you notice? What are the people feeling?

- If you were in the picture, where would you be? What would you be doing? When do you do or see something similar to what is in the picture?

- What do you want to say to God (or Jesus) about this picture?

Older Children and Teens

Set a prayerful atmosphere. Make the sign of the cross, followed by **Thirty Seconds of Silence**.

Seeing. Spend some time viewing the artwork. Ask guiding questions: What is it about? What details do you notice? What is the mood of the artwork? What are the people in the artwork doing? What do their postures and facial expressions say about their feelings? This is a good time to share any relevant information about the artwork that you may have researched, such as the possible motivation or context for the artwork's creation. If the artwork depicts a biblical scene, read the relevant Bible passage.

Meditating. Spend time meditating on how God might be speaking to you through the artwork. Which figure do you most identify with? Why? How would you participate in the scene? Does the artist's depiction of the subject (for example, Jesus, the Virgin Mary, or a scene from the Bible) affirm or challenge the way you thought of the subject previously? If you were the artist, how would you depict the subject differently, and why? What feelings does the art surface in you? What events or issues in your life does it bring to mind? Ask the Holy Spirit to guide you as you silently meditate on these questions.

Responding. How does the artwork call you to respond? Pray your response, either out loud with the group, or silently.

An excellent resource to help teens and older children prayerfully meditate on art is *Beyond the Written Word: Exploring Faith Through Christian Art* by Eileen M. Daily (Saint Mary's Press, 2005).

Learn More
CCC, 1159–1162; 2501–2503
Letter to Artists (a letter written by Pope John Paul II available at the Vatican website, vatican.va)

Meditative Prayer

Meditation is one of the three "expressions of prayer" described by the *Catechism* (the others are **Vocal Prayer** and **Contemplative Prayer**). Meditative prayer involves considering something holy in order to grow closer to God. It is usually aided by imaginative thought (imagining Christ's birth or passion, for instance), by reading sacred texts or Scripture, or gazing on artwork.

There are many different forms of meditation; some mentioned elsewhere in this chapter include: **Bite-sized Biblical Prayers, Daily Examen, Eucharistic Adoration, Lectio Divina, Meditate on Art, Prayer Inspired by Nature, Pray the Our Father Meditatively, Pray the Rosary, Stations of the Cross**.

The Catholic Diocese of Townsville, Australia, offers a comprehensive website on teaching meditation and contemplation to children at cominghome.org.au.

Learn More
CCC, 2705–2708

Memorizing Prayers

The easiest way to help your kids memorize basic prayers such as the Hail Mary, Our Father, and Apostles' Creed is to pray them together on a regular basis. Choose one prayer to pray for a month or two; pray it out loud, slowly and clearly, even if you're the only one saying the prayer. Eventually, even the youngest children will begin to join in.

If you want to be more proactive about memorizing prayers, try the following tips:

Provide an incentive. Create a sticker chart to track your child's progress, or buy some mini M&Ms and offer one for each line memorized.

Break it down on flash cards. Print the prayer out on flash cards, one line per card. (Use pictures or symbols for children who can't read yet.) Begin by having your child arrange the cards in the proper order. Then have him try saying the prayer one line at a time, using the cards as prompts. Eventually, have the child say the prayer from memory, relying on the cards only as necessary.

Repetition is key. Say or read the first line of the prayer together, then have the child repeat it on his own until he is able to repeat it flawlessly. Do the same with the second line by itself, then try repeating both together.

Keep practice sessions short. Keep practice sessions to five or ten minutes a day; longer periods are less effective.

Talking Points: Why Memorize Prayers?

If your kids ask why they have to memorize prayers, here are three good responses:

Connecting with the Church. Memorized prayer helps us pray with the rest of the Church, especially during public liturgies such as the Mass. Plus, sharing the same basic prayers connects us with Christians around the world and throughout history.

A mental prayer book. Memorizing prayers provides us with a sort of "mental prayer book" that we can draw on later in life, especially during times of stress or crisis, when more spontaneous prayer might be impossible.

Traditional prayers are tried and true. Traditional prayers, especially the Our Father, teach us to pray by providing tried-and-true formulations, and they often contain a wisdom that goes beyond our own.

See **Pray the Our Father Meditatively** for another approach to memorizing traditional prayers.

Learn More
CCC, 2688
General Directory for Catechesis, 154

Novenas

When you are going through a time of great difficulty or suffering, or when you want to pray for an intention with special urgency and intensity, your family might consider praying a novena.

Novenas are a traditional pious devotion in which special prayers are said for nine consecutive days, often for the intercession of a saint, the Virgin Mary, or one of the persons of the

Trinity. There are hundreds of traditional novenas; you can find these novenas in a prayer book or by searching online. (Find this article on pbgrace.com for some links.)

Some popular novenas to try: Novena to the Sacred Heart of Jesus, Novena to Christ the King, Novena to the Holy Spirit (Pentecost Novena), Novena to Our Lady of Perpetual Help, Novena to the Immaculate Conception, Novena to St. Nicholas, Novena to St. Patrick, Novena to St. Jude, Novena to St. Francis of Assisi, Novena of Grace, All Souls' Novena, Christmas Novena.

Younger Children
You can introduce younger children to this practice by using Good Deed Beads (see pbgrace.com), **Paper Chain Prayers**, or a chart or calendar to track the number of days of the novena. Keep the prayer simple; you might use a prayer your children already know, or make up a kid-friendly prayer of your own.

Talking Points: The Ancient Roots of the Novena
The novena has its roots in the Greek and Roman practice of spending nine days in mourning following a death. Early converts to Christianity translated that tradition into nine days of prayer, drawing on the nine days that the Virgin Mary and the apostles prayed in the upper room between Christ's Ascension and the descent of the Holy Spirit.

Pray for the Dead

Remember to pray for the dead on All Souls' Day (November 2), when passing a cemetery, or on the anniversary of the death of friends and relatives.

Keep a calendar of the death dates of deceased relatives. (The Church typically celebrates saints' feast days on the anniversary of their death, which also marks their birth into new life.)

Set out pictures or other mementos of deceased friends and relatives on the anniversary of their death.

Use the Eternal Rest prayer found in **A Handful of Catholic Prayers** at the back of this book, or go to pbgrace.com for more possibilities.

Talking Points: Why We Pray for the Dead
The practice of praying for the dead dates back at least as far as a couple centuries before Christ (see 2 Maccabees 12:38–46) and has long been part of the Christian tradition. The Church teaches that the souls of those who die in friendship with God but who are not completely purified of sin are assured eternal salvation, but must first undergo a final purification from sin ("purgatory") in order to enter the joy of heaven (see *CCC*, 1030–1031). We pray for the dead to help them with this purification, to remember them, and to honor them. After all, as Christians we believe that our relationship with friends and relatives is not severed by death, only changed.

Learn More
CCC, 1032

Pray the Five Forms of Prayer

As an expression of our friendship with God, prayer should be rich and varied. One way to vary your family prayer is to practice praying the five forms of prayer listed in the *Catechism*: blessing and adoration, petition, intercession, thanksgiving, and praise.

Catholic Household Blessings and Prayers contains dozens of prayers in each of these categories, but here are some general ideas.

Blessing and Adoration

We are able to bless God because he has blessed us first (see *CCC*, 2645). The psalms offer many examples of blessing prayer: "Bless the Lord, O my soul, and do not forget all his benefits . . . who satisfies you with good as long as you live" (Psalm 103:2, 5). Blessing is closely related to adoration, which is an expression of love for God.

- Sing or pray the psalms. (See **Sing Your Prayer**.)

- Practice **Eucharistic Adoration**.

Petition

Petitionary prayer asks God to provide what we need. "Forgiveness, the quest for the Kingdom, and every true need are objects of the prayer of petition" *(CCC, 2646)*.

Pray the Our Father, which contains the fundamental elements of petitionary prayer in its requests for the coming of God's kingdom, our daily needs, and the forgiveness of our sins.

Do an **Examination of Conscience**, and then offer a general prayer asking God's forgiveness.

Encourage kids to place prayers of petition in **God's Mailbox**, or to write them in a **Prayer Journal**.

Intercession

Prayer of intercession asks God to provide what is good for other people, particularly our enemies (see *CCC,* 2647). The Universal Prayer (or General Intercessions) we say at Mass is an example of intercessory prayer.

- Keep a list of your prayer intentions on the refrigerator, or in some other public place. See **List Your Prayer Intentions.**

- Pray intercessory prayers in the responsorial style used during Mass: "For (intention), let us pray to the Lord; Lord, hear our prayer" (or another suitable response).

- Try to think of a broad range of intercessory prayers: for members of your family, friends and neighbors, community members, the sick and poor and lonely, those affected by conflict or unjust situations, the Church, and political leaders. You can find suggestions for intercessory prayers in *Catholic Household Blessings and Prayers.*

Thanksgiving

Prayer of thanksgiving flows from the recognition that everything is a gift from God. Nurturing an "attitude of gratitude" helps us see everything as gift—even our sorrows and suffering (see *CCC,* 2648).

- Keep a **Gratitude Journal** (or a wall poster for posting "thankful thoughts").

- Practice **Highs and Lows** or a **Daily Examen** in order to better recognize and name God's gifts.

Praise

"Prayer of praise is entirely disinterested and rises to God, lauds him, and gives him glory for his own sake, quite beyond what he has done, but simply because HE IS" (*CCC,* 2649).

- Sing a song of praise; see **Sing Your Prayer**, below.

- Practice praising God spontaneously; invoke the help of the Holy Spirit to speak through your prayer.

- You can also listen to songs of praise while in the car or even around the house, letting your spirit silently join the words of the singer.

Learn More
CCC, 2626–2649

Pray the Our Father Meditatively

The Our Father (or Lord's Prayer) is the preeminent prayer for Christians because it is the prayer Jesus gave his disciples when they asked him to teach them how to pray.

You can open up the meaning and beauty of this prayer for your kids by praying it meditatively, using one of the following approaches:

Pray it with the *Catechism*. Read a paragraph of the commentary on the Our Father found in the *Catechism* (2759–2865) before praying the Our Father, eventually working your way through the entire commentary.

Use books and videos. Try another resource for meditating on the Our Father, such as the video meditation provided by Maryknoll or *Praying as Jesus Taught Us: Meditations on the Our Father* by Cardinal Carlo Maria Martini (Sheed & Ward, 2001). You can find additional resources at pbgrace.com.

Paraphrase the meaning for kids. If you are using the flashcard method of helping young children memorize the Our Father (see **Memorizing Prayers**), summarize the meaning of each line in kid-friendly language in smaller print on each card.

Learn More
CCC, 2759–2865

Pray the Rosary

The rosary is one of the most recognizable of Catholic prayers. If you haven't prayed the rosary before, you will find a basic description and "how to" guide in **A Handful of Catholic Prayers** at the back of this book.

If you have been reluctant to pray the rosary because it seemed too simplistic or Mary-centered, check out the ***Talking Points*** section below for some reasons to give it a try.

Here are some strategies for praying the rosary with kids.

Younger Children

Skip the beads, or get kid-friendly ones. If you're praying with children too young to follow direction, say the rosary without the aid of rosary beads. (Very young children may end up whipping them around.) When your kids are old enough, purchase a durable, kid-friendly rosary, such as a cord rosary.

Start with one decade. Praying one decade of the rosary should take a little longer than five minutes. Be sure to introduce the mystery in advance; meditate on a different mystery each time, so that you eventually work your way through all the mysteries.

Shorten the decades. Say the entire rosary, but only say three Hail Mary prayers for each decade. This is a good way of introducing your children to the order of the mysteries and the rhythm of the entire rosary; plan on spending about fifteen minutes.

Use pictures to aid meditation. Find pictures (online or in a book) illustrating each mystery of the rosary. Display the pictures as you briefly explain and then pray each mystery. Or check out *The Illuminated Rosary* series at pbgrace.com/rosary; each book contains works of sacred art illuminating a different set of mysteries; young children can follow the rosary by looking at the pictures (one per bead), and older children can use it to help them learn the prayers.

Set a prayerful mood. Before you begin the rosary, set the mood with **Smells and Bells**, singing a Marian hymn, or practicing **Thirty Seconds of Silence**.

Ignore the kids and pray. If your children act up while you're praying, ignore them as best you can and pray the rosary yourself. Someday, your kids will "grow into" the practice, and in the meantime, Mary, mother of us all, surely sympathizes.

Older Children and Teens
In addition to the ideas above, consider the following:

Make your own cord rosaries. Teens have been crafting their own knotted and dyed rosaries from nylon cord since the 1980s; you can find supplies and instructions at Rosary Army (rosaryarmy.newevangelizers.com).

Pray the Scriptural rosary. As the name implies, the Scriptural rosary incorporates very brief, relevant Scripture readings before each Hail Mary; for example, the first joyful mystery, the Annunciation, would be interspersed with lines from Luke 1, taking the reader through the Biblical account of the Annunciation. You can purchase a Scriptural rosary book, or find different versions online.

Look for cool supplemental resources. There is a wealth of resources available that might enhance your teen's experience of the rosary, from rosary music CDs to books of reflections on the mysteries written by teens.

Talking Points: Why Pray the Rosary?
In the rosary, we ask Mary to "pray for us sinners"—in other words, to join us in our prayer. Mary is "favored" by God and "blessed among women," according to the angel Gabriel (Luke 1:28), because of the role she plays in fulfilling God's plan of salvation. So reciting the Hail Mary—a prayer rooted in the Gospel

of Luke—makes sense: We ask Mary to join us in our prayer just as we would ask any close friend to pray with us, but Mary is much more than just another friend; Jesus appointed her as our "spiritual mother" (John 19:27).

At the same time, the rosary is a profoundly Christ-centered prayer. When we ask Mary to accompany us in praying the rosary, she leads us to Jesus (see John 2:5). As we recite the prayers that make up the rosary (the Our Father, the Hail Mary, the Glory Be), we also meditate on the "mysteries" of God's plan of salvation as described in the Gospels: the announcement of Jesus' birth, his ministry, his Passion, his Resurrection and Ascension, and so on. (There are twenty mysteries of the rosary in all.)

As even this brief explanation suggests, the rosary is a complex, multilayered form of prayer. On one level, the repetition of its vocal prayers makes it accessible even to children, as does the sensory aspect of fingering the rosary beads. But it is also a form of meditation, and when intentions are offered prior to each mystery, it also becomes a form of petitionary or intercessory prayer. Finally, the call-and-response rhythm of the prayers when the rosary is said in a group joins our prayers together to become the prayer of the whole Body of Christ, the Church.

Learn More

Luke 1:26–56

CCC, 963–976; 2673–2679

The Rosary of the Virgin Mary (Rosarium Virginis Mariae), an apostolic letter of John Paul II available at the Vatican website, vatican.va

Pray for the Sick

Take a moment to think about the rituals you go through when a family member gets sick: breaking out the thermometer, giving medicine, making chicken noodle soup or green tea, and so on. Why not add prayer to the mix? After all, healing was a centerpiece of Jesus' ministry, and he commanded the apostles to heal the sick as well (see Mark 16:17–18).

- Prepare ahead of time by keeping holy water in your medicine cabinet, along with a prayer for sickness. You can find numerous prayers for and blessings of the sick in *Catholic Household Blessings and Prayers*.

- Gather around the sick person and lay hands on him or her, in keeping with Jesus' command.

- If a family member is seriously ill, about to have surgery, or in danger of death, check with your parish about having her receive the sacrament of Anointing. Once popularly referred to as "Last Rites," the sacrament of Anointing isn't just for people on the point of death (see *CCC*, 1514). See **Celebrate the Anointing of the Sick**.

Learn More
CCC, 1500–1510
Mark 6:12–13; Mark 16:17–18; James 5:14–15

Pray Traditional Prayers and Devotions

Catholics have an enormous library of prayer, collected from around the world over thousands of years. Try some of these traditional prayers every so often during your **Family Prayer Time**. You will find a few in **A Handful of Catholic Prayers** at the back of this book, and links to more at pbgrace.com.

Pray When You Pass a Church

A tradition being revived in some families is the practice of saying a quick prayer—typically the Sign of the Cross or a short exhortation such as "Jesus, we love you!"—when passing a Catholic Church, in acknowledgment of Jesus' real presence in the form of the Eucharist in the church's tabernacle.

For **Talking Points** related to this practice, see **Eucharistic Adoration**.

Prayer Inspired by Nature

The next time you enjoy outdoor recreation (whether on a camping trip or just in your backyard), let wonder of the natural world inspire your family to pray.

Here are a few ideas for using nature as an inspiration for prayer:

Bless and praise God for his creation. *Catholic Household Blessings and Prayers* contains several blessings and prayers related to nature; see the Blessing of Animals, the Blessing of the Products of Nature, and the Canticle of the Sun (Prayer of St. Francis). The Bible also contains numerous songs of praise inspired by creation. A few examples include Genesis 1:1—2:3; Genesis 9:8-13; Psalm 104; Psalm 148; Job 38-39; and Daniel 3:52-90. Teens might also explore the poetry of Jesuit priest Gerard Manley Hopkins, particularly "The Windhover," "Pied Beauty," and "God's Grandeur."

Lectio divina. Follow the method of meditative prayer known as *Lectio divina*, using the natural world around you as a "text." For the first step, spend time "reading" your environment by either actively exploring it or by being still and quietly observing. (Search for "nature sit spots" online for details on the growing "sport" of quietly observing the natural world from a single location.) Share your observations with one another: What did you see? What did you hear? Then move through the other steps of *Lectio divina* to prayerfully meditate on the meaning of what you "read." See **Lectio Divina** for more about this prayer practice.

Examen. Use the Ignatian **Daily Examen** to reflect on how you encountered the presence of God in the natural world.

Collect a bouquet. Collect flowers, pinecones, pebbles, shells, feathers, or other natural objects that show God's glory and present them to God (or the Virgin Mary, or one of the saints) in a spirit of gratitude by placing them in your **Home Oratory**.

Read the stories of saints who befriended God's creatures. The next time you are sitting around the campfire, read the story of a saint whose love of God was expressed in his or her love of God's creation. Saint Francis of Assisi is an obvious example, but Ethel Pochocki proposes other animal- and nature-loving saints in her kid-friendly *Once Upon a Time Saints* series: Comgall (friend of swans and mice); Felix (friend of spiders); Hubert (protector of deer); Kentigern (brought a bird back to life); Martin de Porres (veterinarian and friend of animals, especially mice); Melangell (protector of wildlife, especially rabbits); Pharaildis (friend of animals, restored a dead goose); and Rigobert (befriended a goose), to name a few. At the end of the story, incorporate the saint into a prayer of gratitude for the beauty of God's creation.

Talking Points: Meeting God in the Natural World
Use your time outdoors to share the Church's teaching about the environment with your children. Here are some talking points:

We can encounter God in nature. Since ancient times, the natural world has been one of the ways that people come to know about God and experience his wisdom and glory (*CCC*, 32, 299; *Compendium of the Social Doctrine of the Church*, 487). Many of the saints lived in harmony with the natural world and had special friendships with animals as a consequence of their closeness to God (see the partial list above).

We still need the Church. Your older kids might ask: "If we can encounter God in nature, why do we need the Church? Why can't nature be our church?" It is important for them to understand that the Church isn't just another human organization; rather, it is both a sign of our communion with God and the unity of the human race, and the means by which our union with God and other people is accomplished (*CCC*, 775). Catholics say that the Church is the sacrament of Christ—the means by which Christ is physically manifested in the world, and by which he continues his saving work. So even though the beauty of the night sky or the mystery of life unfolding in a stream might lift our minds to God, it is only in the Church that we are saved from the power of sin and death (see *CCC*, 846–847).

God intends creation for our good. Our faith teaches us to treat our natural environment within the context of God's overall plan of salvation (see *Compendium*, 451). God intends the created world to serve the good of human beings, who are the "summit" of his creation (see *CCC*, 343). The Church rejects any view that values the environment as much as or more than human beings, or makes creation into a sort of god. We are called to care for creation in part to preserve it for the benefit of all human beings, including future generations (see *CCC*, 2416).

God calls on us to respect creation for its own sake. The Church also rejects views that reduce the natural world to something to be manipulated and exploited (see *Compendium*, 463). Creation has its own intrinsic value, for the simple reason that God made it and called it "good" (Genesis 1); God loves and cares for each of his creatures (see *CCC*, 342), so we should, too.

Learn More
CCC, 282–301, 337–349, 846–847, 2415–2418
Compendium of the Social Doctrine of the Church, "Chapter Ten: Safeguarding the Environment," 451–487

Sacred Story Time

Teach your children how to prayerfully reflect on sacred texts by using the basic movements of *lectio divina* as you read from a children's picture Bible or a children's book of the saints.

Lectio divina, or "sacred reading," is an ancient method of praying with sacred texts that dates to the fourth century. Usually the text comes from the Scriptures, but other texts may be used as well, such as the writings of the saints. *Lectio divina* takes many forms, but traditionally it is divided into four steps: *lectio* (reading), *meditatio* (meditation), *oratio* (prayer), and *contemplatio* (contemplation).

When you read sacred stories with your children slowly, pausing to pray and talk about what God is saying through the story, you provide them with skills and habits for reading the Bible and other sacred texts more fruitfully as they grow older.

Here is one way to practice "sacred reading" with your children:

1. Reading. Use a short story (the shorter the better, but definitely less than five minutes long) from a good picture Bible, a Bible-based storybook, or a children's book about the lives of the saints. Help your child prepare to hear the story by allowing a short settling down time, and explaining what you're going to do: "Now let's read a story about God. While I read, you listen for what God is doing in the story." Don't worry about questions or interruptions: if they are about the text, then your child is already "meditating" on it; if not, address the distraction and gently redirect attention back to the story. You may want to read the story or parts of the story again, either immediately or during a later step.

2. Meditation. If your child doesn't have questions or comments of her own, offer some comments and prompting questions: What is happening in the picture (or in the story)? Why? What are characters thinking or feeling? How is God acting in this story? (If God isn't directly mentioned in the story, you may need to suggest some ways that God is quietly present.) Which character would you like to be? What would you do differently if you were that character? How would you feel?

3. Prayer. Invite your child to respond to the story in prayer: "You know, God gives us stories like this to help us grow closer to him. Let's pray to God about this story. What would you like to say to God? Or what questions do you want to ask God about this story?" Provide guiding prompts, if necessary. Be sure to offer your own prayer response, both to make the experience prayerful for you and to model prayer for your child.

4. Listening. With young children, the contemplation step can be described as listening to God: "Now that we've prayed to God about this story, let's be quiet so we can hear what God might be saying back to us, inside our hearts." Take at least thirty seconds to be silent. If your child is restless or noisy, do your best to complete the period of silence yourself.

5. Wrapping up. You can finish by asking your child whether he heard God speaking to him. If he says no, you can reassure him that it's okay—sometimes we aren't listening closely enough, and sometimes God just likes to spend time quietly with us. End by blessing your child. (See **Bless One Another**.) For ways of adapting this practice for older kids and teens, see the main **Lectio Divina** article.

Saint Prayers

The next time you pray with your family, consider inviting a few friends to pray with you . . . not just any friends, but the women, children, and men who pray face-to-face with God because of their perfect union with him.

These special friends are the saints, of course, and Catholics don't hesitate to ask for their prayers. (If you or your kids wonder about this practice, see the *Talking Points* section below.)

Start out by asking St. Anthony to intercede for your kids when they lose important things around the house. Branch out to other saints by learning the patron saints associated with various causes and issues. Here is a brief sampling:

- Animals: St. Francis, St. Martin de Porres

- Children: St. Nicholas

- Computers and the Internet: St. Isidore of Seville, St. Anthony of Padua

- Impossible causes: St. Jude, St. Frances Xavier Cabrini

- Kids with behavior problems and kids who feel like outcasts: St. Dominic Savio

- Students: St. Thomas Aquinas, St. Catherine of Alexandria, Saint Benedict

- Musicians: St. Cecilia

- Orphans and abandoned children: St. Jerome Emiliani

- Teenagers: St. Aloysius Gonzaga, St. Maria Goretti

Talking Points: Why Pray with the Saints?

Some people object to the Catholic practice of asking for the prayers of the saints. Usually, this objection rests on the fact that Christians have one mediator and intercessor in Jesus Christ.

Catholics affirm this basic truth, but also recognize that it is part of God's plan for all of humanity to participate in his saving work. This is why he chose the Israelites to be the instrument of his salvation for the world, and why Jesus gathered a community of friends to share in his work rather than doing it all himself. Christians are initiated into this work through their baptism, by which they share in the redemptive suffering, death, and Resurrection of Jesus Christ. They continue sharing in God's saving work by offering their daily lives—all their joys and sufferings and sacrifices—for God's purposes.

This work doesn't end when people die. If anything, those who die in friendship with God are able to participate more fully in his work.

Another way to think of it is this: If you have ever prayed for someone else, or asked someone else to pray for you, what you were doing is no different than what we ask the saints to do for us.

Learn More

CCC, 2683–2684

Sing Your Prayer

The *Catechism of the Catholic Church* quotes St. Augustine as saying, "He who sings prays twice" (1157), and St. Paul urges Christians to "be filled with the Spirit, as you sing psalms and hymns and spiritual songs among yourselves, singing and making melody to the Lord in your hearts, giving thanks to God the Father at all times and for everything in the name of our Lord Jesus Christ" (Ephesians 5:18–20).

If your family likes to sing, there is no reason why you can't incorporate that love of music into your prayer time. Here are some ways to begin:

Sing what you already know. Think of religious hymns or songs you know by heart. Simple liturgical responses from the Mass, such as a sung "Amen" or "Alleluia" would be a good starting place for incorporating song into your **Family Prayer Time**.

Learn church music. Purchase or borrow your parish's hymnal and sing your favorite "church songs" together. Try to learn the most common ones by heart, to make sung participation in the Mass easier.

Sing along to popular religious music. Purchase religious children's music and learn the more prayerful songs with your child. (See pbgrace.com for suggestions.)

Add an instrument, start a band. If anyone in your family plays an instrument, have him play along. Give younger children kid-friendly instruments (shakers, jingle bell sticks, clappers, tambourines, etc.) to help them "make a joyful noise to the Lord" (Psalm 100:1).

Learn More
CCC, 1157–1158

Smells and Bells

The Catholic liturgy is sometimes said to be one of "smells and bells," a reference to the use of incense, candles, scented oil, altar bells (sanctus bells), elaborate vestments, and other elements that engage the senses. Incorporate some of those elements into your own **Family Prayer Time**:

Candles. Make and use prayer candles to set aside your time of prayer, and to indicate different liturgical seasons. (See **Prayer Candle** for details.)

Bells. Use a hand-held bell or other appropriate musical instruments to call children to prayer.

Incense. During special times of prayer, consider burning incense. The use of incense to accompany prayer dates to ancient times (Psalm 141:2 refers to it), symbolizing sanctification, purification, and the prayers of the faithful rising to heaven. Myrrh resin (the type of incense burned in churches) can be purchased from Catholic supply retailers.

Holy water. A reminder of our baptism into Christ, holy water can be incorporated into your prayers and blessings (see **Holy Water**).

Tablecloth or banner. Use colored cloth to make a tablecloth or banner for your **Home Oratory**, and change them as appropriate for each liturgical feast or season.

Other symbols. Use other sacred or symbolic objects, as appropriate: icons, crucifixes, flowers, and so on. See **Home Oratory** for more suggestions.

Talking Points: Why Smells and Bells?

Why do Catholics have all these "smells and bells"? The *Catechism* offers this simple answer: "As a being at once body and spirit, man expresses and perceives spiritual realities through physical signs and symbols. As a social being, man needs signs and symbols to communicate with others, through language, gestures, and actions. The same holds true for his relationship with God" (1146).

Learn More
CCC, 1145–1152

Stations of the Cross

Since the earliest centuries of the Church, Christians have made pilgrimages to Jerusalem in order to retrace the steps of Jesus during his suffering and death (the *Via Dolorosa* or "Way of Sorrow"). Around the fifteenth century, Christians began the practice of prayerfully meditating on the Passion of Christ by reproducing that pilgrimage in miniature in what eventually became known as the Stations of the Cross.

Today there are fourteen stations, each of which represents an event during Christ's passion. Besides the traditional Stations, St. John Paul II introduced a form of the Stations more closely linked to events recorded in the Scriptures; this form of the Stations is known as the Scriptural Stations of the Cross. You will find a list of the Stations of the Cross in **A Handful of Catholic Prayers** at the end of this book.

Here are some ways to pray the Stations of the Cross with your family:

Find a public service. Join a public meditation on the Stations of the Cross at a local parish or retreat center; these are most common during Lent and other penitential times.

Pray the Stations as a family at your parish. Most Catholic parishes have the Stations of the Cross depicted in pictures or bas relief on the side walls of the nave, or sometimes on the grounds outdoors. Pick a quiet time to visit the church to say the Stations there.

Find the guide that fits your family. For a richer experience of the Stations of the Cross, find a meditation guide to deepen your prayer and reflection. *Catholic Household Blessings and Prayers* contains one such guide, but there are literally hundreds in circulation. You can find them at your parish, a bookstore, or online (go to pbhrace.com for links). If you have young children, look for a Stations of the Cross geared toward their age.

Say the Stations of the Cross at home. If you do the Stations of the Cross at home, hang pictures representing each station around the house, making your own "Way of the Cross." The pictures can be printed out (search online for images tagged "Stations of the Cross"), or you can have your older children draw them.

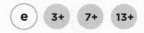

Thirty Seconds of Silence

Prepare for **Mealtime Prayers** or **Family Prayer** with thirty seconds of silence, a practice that helps everyone (including parents) settle down and refocus their attention. It also helps children learn to be silent and still, which is good preparation for other prayer practices, such as meditative or contemplative prayer.

Here's what to do:

- Explain that you will be spending this time in silent prayer. You might encourage younger children to listen for the presence of God, or for what Jesus is whispering in their hearts.

- Optionally, light a **Prayer Candle** as a way of signaling that this is a special time, and as a sign of God's presence.

- Start with thirty seconds and gradually lengthen the time.

- Model prayerful silence by spending the time actually opening yourself to the presence of God. As much as possible, ignore children's fidgeting and giggling (at least during the time of silence). With enough practice, even young children will begin to imitate your example.

Learn More
CCC, 2717
1 Kings 19:12; Psalm 62:5

Vocal Prayer

Vocal prayer is one of the three "expressions of prayer" named in the *Catechism of the Catholic Church,* along with meditation and contemplation.

Although Jesus often prayed silently, he also gave voice to his prayer. He offered blessings and thanks to the Father, petitioned the Father during his agony in the garden of Gethsemane, and taught his disciples to pray the Our Father. In both his interior prayer and his vocal prayer, Jesus gave his followers a model of how to pray.

You, too, can use vocal prayer to teach your kids to pray—not only by reciting a text or memorized prayer out loud, but also by praying more spontaneously as part of your ongoing conversation with God. Occasionally bringing your spontaneous prayer "out in the open" offers your kids a model that might inspire their own conversations with God.

Talking Points: Why Pray Out Loud?
The *Catechism* offers this beautiful introduction to its discussion of vocal prayer: "Through his Word [Christ], God speaks to man. By words, mental or vocal, our prayer takes flesh" (2700).

This "taking flesh" in our spoken words is an especially human way to pray; as not only spiritual but also bodily beings, we need to involve our whole being in prayer, including our voices (see *CCC*, 2702).

Learn more:
CCC, 2700–2704

Write Your Prayer

Many people find that the process of writing down their thoughts helps clarify their prayer, much as journaling can help people clarify their thoughts and feelings. You can encourage older kids and teens to write down their prayers of petition, blessing, gratitude, intercession, and praise (see **Pray the Five Form of Prayer**). Alternatively, they can jot down their thoughts and reflections as part of their meditative prayer; try incorporating writing into the meditative aspects of the **Daily Examen** and **Lectio Divina**.

Here are some other ways to incorporate writing into your family prayer:

Notecards to God. Purchase blank index cards (or inexpensive notecards) for your kids to write short prayers on every day, or as they feel moved throughout the day; they can "send" them to God by leaving them in **God's Mailbox** or in your **Home Oratory**. Written prayers might also be displayed on a bulletin board, or on your refrigerator.

Prayer journal. Teens may wish to keep a prayer journal, not only as a way of praying to God, but also as a way of reflecting on their prayer life. See the **Prayer Journal** article for ideas.

Write a psalm. If you are in the habit of regularly reading and praying the psalms with your older kids, encourage them to write their own psalm, using their own words to express their deepest feelings of sadness, loneliness, anger, joy, or praise in the form of a song to God.

Collect prayers. You can encourage kids to collect their favorite prayers by writing them down; see **Make a Book of Prayers** for ideas.

CHAPTER FOUR

Helps for Praying Together

Advent Wreath

Observe Advent (the period of four weeks before Christmas) with the help of an Advent wreath. Advent wreaths consist of four candles, three violet and one rose, set in a circular wreath. One candle is lit for each Sunday of Advent, with the rose candle being lit on the third Sunday (Gaudete Sunday, from the Latin word for "rejoice").

Here are some ideas for praying with an Advent wreath:

Make your own Advent wreath. If you do not own an Advent wreath, make your own as a family. You can use this activity as a time to talk about Advent and the symbolism of the wreath. You'll find instructions for making all sorts of Advent wreaths online; see pbgrace.com for links.

Bless your Advent wreath, Nativity scene, and Christmas tree. The U.S. Catholic bishops provide blessings for Advent wreaths, Nativity scenes (mangers), and Christmas trees at their website and in *Catholic Household Blessings and Prayers*.

Sing Advent songs. "O Come, O Come, Emmanuel" is an ancient hymn traditionally sung during Advent. Look through your parish's hymnal for other Advent hymns to sing.

Chant or read the O Antiphons. The O Antiphons are short, chanted prayers that are traditionally prayed in the evening during the last seven days of Advent (from December 17 through 23). You can find the O Antiphons in *Catholic Household Blessings and Prayers* and at the website of the U.S. Catholic bishops, usccb.org.

Use Advent prayer resources. Catholic parishes typically offer a wealth of Advent prayer resources for free or a small fee. You can find additional resources at most major Catholic publishers' websites, the USCCB website, and pbgrace.com.

Learn More
CCC, 524

Apps for Prayer

If you're a tech-connected family, load up your cell phone (or your teen's cell phone) with the latest Catholic prayer apps, of which there are dozens. Some examples:

- Laudate is a popular, free Catholic prayer app that offers daily Mass readings, the Liturgy of the Hours, rosary, stations of the cross, daily meditations, and more.

- Art/y/fact helps users interpret and meditate on Christian art.

- 3-Minute Retreat, from Loyola Press, offers a daily

three-minute retreat featuring music, Scripture verses, and reflective thoughts and questions.

- Steubenville Youth Conferences App serves up videos of speakers and music from the Steubenville Youth Conferences, but also allows users to connect with one another by posting prayer requests.

- You can find many more possibilities at CatholicApps.com.

Display Holy Images and Objects

Display sacred images and objects in your home as a constant reminder of God's presence. Examples of items to display include icons, crucifixes, small statues, baptismal candles, and religious artwork (modern or classical). These can be displayed throughout the house or in a prayer corner (see **Home Oratory**).

Among the items to consider placing in your child's bedroom: a print of Jesus welcoming the children; a crucifix; a religious nightlight (such as an angel); or a **Prayer Pillow**.

Talking Points: Why Do Catholics Display Sacred Images?
The use of material objects for holy purposes is rooted in the fact that Christ became physically present to us in his Incarnation and chose to continue being physically present to us through the sacraments. It makes sense that God would want to encounter us physically, since he made us physical beings who perceive the world primarily through sight, hearing, touch, taste, and smell. As the Church says, because of Christ's pas-

sion, death, and resurrection, "there is scarcely any proper use of material things which cannot be . . . directed toward the sanctification of men and the praise of God" (*Sacrosanctum Concilium*, 61).

Objects blessed for holy purposes can never be considered magical; they are simply reserved as tools to help us grow closer to God. Similarly, when Catholics use sacred images (such as icons or statues) for prayer, they honor the person depicted by the image, not the image itself (*CCC*, 2132).

Learn More
CCC, 1159–1162

God's Mailbox

Decorate a cardboard box (or buy a wood mailbox and decorate it) with the words "God's Mailbox" and place it in your **Home Oratory** or on a wall. Provide notecards for kids to write or draw their prayers on, either during **Family Prayer Time** or anytime they feel so moved.

Kids can "send" their prayers to God by dropping them in the mailbox. Optionally, collect the notecards into a memory book for your kids to browse when they are older.

Older Children and Teens
Older children and teens may like to try a variation on this idea by writing a note to God and sending it to Jerusalem to be placed in the Western Wall of the Temple Mount. According to Jewish tradition, God's presence has never moved from

the Western Wall, which is part of the old wall surrounding the Temple courtyard. About a million notes are placed in the cracks and crevices of the wall every year; twice a year, they are collected by the Rabbi of the Western Wall and buried in the Jewish cemetery on the Mount of Olives. Pope John Paul II and Pope Benedict XVI, among other dignitaries, have left notes in the Western Wall.

Notes can be mailed to the Western Wall in Jerusalem, or sent electronically via english.thekotel.org; notes sent electronically are printed out and placed in the wall.

Gratitude or Thanksgiving Journal

Gratitude for God's goodness is the foundation of Christian prayer. In fact, the word Eucharist is Greek for "thanksgiving." Here are some ideas for praying with gratitude:

Gratitude journal. Practice gratitude by keeping a list or journal of all that your family is thankful for, incorporating the process into your family meal or prayer time. If your kids have trouble coming up with new things to be thankful for, try doing **Highs and Lows** first.

Make a thanksgiving mural. For younger children, set aside some wall space (or window space, using dry erase markers) for posting words of gratitude. Get creative and make a mural—for example, a tree in which the leaves are prayers of thanks, a rainbow with raindrops of thanks, etc.

Dedicate the month of November to thanksgiving. Many families place a special emphasis on making a long list of things to be thankful for during the month leading up to the Thanksgiving holiday. Bring the list to your Thanksgiving meal to read.

#thankful. Make your attitude of gratitude public by sharing your list on social media.

Learn More
Psalm 136:1; Luke 17:11–19; 1 Thessalonians 5:18
CCC, 2637–2638

Grab-Bag Prayers

Give children a small leadership role during prayer time by letting them choose the prayers. You can provide some boundaries by making up a fun system for doing this. Here are a few ideas:

Bookmarked prayers. Use bookmarks or Post-It Flags to mark appropriate prayers in your family prayer book; let children choose from the bookmarked prayers. Write the name of the prayer on the bookmark, or use drawings or symbols for children who cannot read.

Sticks. Print photos of friends and relatives, cut out their faces, place them on craft sticks, and place the sticks in a pot to create a bouquet of friends and family. Have your child choose a different person to pray for every night.

Dice. Find a large block of wood or foam and glue prayers (such as meal prayers or bedtime prayers) to it; have your child roll the die to select the prayer.

Jar. Print out some prayers on heavy cardstock and place them in a jar; have your child pick from the jar without looking. When you print out the prayers, include a picture for children who can't yet read.

Clothespins. Purchase multicolored clothespins and hang them on a line of colorful twine attached to the wall (or on your prayer table). Print out prayers on cardstock and attach them to the line using the clothespins.

Holy Card Key Chain

Want to distract little kids during Mass while introducing them to the saints at the same time? Get a bunch of holy cards, laminate them (if they aren't already laminated), hole-punch them, and throw them on a key chain. Toddlers can play with them instead of your real keys during Mass; as they grow older, you can use the pictures to tell them about the saints. Older kids can use the prayers on the back of the cards as an aid to prayer after communion. Holy cards can be purchased from most Catholic retailers.

Holy Water

Keep holy water in the house to use for special blessings, or keep it in a font near the main door of the house so that people can bless themselves when coming and going. If you have little ones, be sure to keep the holy water font out of their reach to avoid messes.

If you are worried about the water becoming a haven for germs (which can be a real problem if it isn't freshened regularly), add blessed salt to it. (Blessed salt is an ancient sacramental, used especially in the baptismal rite.)

Your parish or pastor will be able to supply you with holy water and blessed salt.

Younger Children and Older Kids

Have younger children and older kids make their own holy water fonts by decorating a glass jar or dish. Use glass paint markers or paper cutouts and glue to decorate the font with appropriate symbols. Alternatively, use air-dry clay to make a font that can be hung on the wall by your door.

Talking Points: The Connection to Baptism

Holy water is a sacramental, a sacred sign that prepares us to receive grace, helps us to cooperate with it, and sets things apart for God (in other words, make them holy).

Holy water recalls the sacrament of baptism. When Catholics bless themselves with holy water, they are recommitting themselves to their baptism and their baptismal mission to make the whole world holy.

It makes sense, then, to bless yourself and your kids with

holy water before leaving the house as a way of strengthening yourselves for your mission.

Learn More
Exodus 14:1; Joshua 3; Mark 1:9-11; Matthew 3:13-17; Matthew 28:19-20; Luke 3:16; John 1:29-33; Acts 2:38; Acts 8:35-38; Acts 16:31, 33; Romans 6:3-6; 1 Corinthians 10:1-2
CCC, 1217-1222, 1238, 1668

Home Oratory (or Prayer Corner)

Set aside a special place in your home for prayer and holy objects—a small table, the mantle above your fireplace, a corner with shelves and comfortable seating. Different families have different names for this kind of space: home altar, home shrine, celebration table, and so on. The *Catechism of the Catholic Church* refers to this home prayer space as a prayer corner or "little oratory." (An oratory is a place of worship not attached to a parish.)

Whatever you call it, use the space as a physical reminder of God's presence in your home, as well as your intention as a family to create "space" for God in your life. You can use the space as the focal point for **Family Prayer Time**, or as a special place for individuals to retreat for prayer or sacred reading. Some objects you might include in your home shrine:

• books for sacred reading and meditation, such as the Bible, children's religious picture books, lives of the saints, a daily missal, prayer books, and so on;

- icons of Jesus, Mary, the Holy Trinity, or the saints;

- candles;

- a tablecloth or covering in colors appropriate for the liturgical season (green, violet, red, white, rose, etc.);

- a crucifix;

- a blessed prayer shawl;

- holy water;

- flowers;

- seasonal objects, such as a rice bowl for Lent and an Advent wreath during Advent.

When installing these objects in your home oratory, you may wish to bless them using the "Prayer for Placing Objects for Prayer and Devotion" found in *Catholic Household Blessings and Prayers*.

For a detailed discussion of home oratories, see *The Little Oratory: A Beginner's Guide to Praying in the Home* by David Clayton and Leila Marie Lawler (Sophia Institute Press, 2014).

Talking Points: Why Keep a Home Oratory?

The Church has long called the family an e*cclesia domestica*, or "domestic church," because it is composed of individuals living out their baptism together. It is fitting, then, for this domestic church to set aside a special place for worship, just as a local church does. The *Catechism* recommends this practice: "In a Christian family, this kind of little oratory fosters prayer in common" (*CCC*, 2691).

For **Talking Points** about the use of sacred images, see **Display Holy Images and Objects**.

Learn More
CCC, 2691

Make a Book of Prayers

As your family tries out different prayers and finds its own favorites, make those prayers your own by collecting them into a family book of prayers.

- Use a blank notebook, journal, or scrapbook to create your family book of prayers. Alternatively, have your kids make their own book by hole-punching pages and tying them together with yarn or string.

- Begin by having your kids copy down prayers they already know.

- As you try out new prayers with your kids (drawing on other prayer books and the Internet), add the ones you especially like to your prayer book.

If this is a practice you keep up over the years, you can provide each of your children with a copy of the book as they leave home.

Paper Chain Prayers

Keep track of your children's prayers with a decorative paper chain. Here's how:

- Cut colored construction paper into strips.

- Every day, have your children write their prayers on one of the strips of paper during their regular prayer time.

- Glue, staple, or tape the strips to make a new link in the chain.

You can use paper chains to pray the five forms of prayer (praise and adoration, petition, intercession, thanksgiving), track your child's progress in learning traditional prayers, pray a novena, or as a gratitude journal. (Check out the related articles for each of these ideas.)

Prayer Candle

Make your **Family Prayer Time** special by lighting a candle.

Make a prayer candle. If this becomes a regular feature of your prayer time, purchase a white pillar candle and decorate it with Christian symbols and words. You will find endless candle decoration ideas online, including instructions for making your own candles from scratch.

Use an electric candle with little ones. If you're worried about mixing an open flame with children, purchase a realistic-looking electric flameless pillar candle.

Use different candles for different seasons. You can buy different colored candles for different liturgical seasons—e.g., purple for Lent, green for Ordinary Time, etc.

Advent wreath. Even if you don't usually use candles during prayer, be sure to light an **Advent Wreath** during the season of Advent.

Talking Points: The Light of Christ
Light is a symbol of Christ (see John 8:12) as well as of his followers (see Matthew 5:14). The practice of lighting candles during prayer reminds us of Christ's presence as well as our call to bring the light of Christ into the world's darkness. This is why, since ancient times, candles have been used in connection with the Easter liturgy, the sacrament of baptism, and the other sacraments.

Learn More
Matthew 5:14–16; John 1:1–9; John 8:12
CCC, 1154, 1189, 1216, 1243

Prayer Journal

Encourage your teen to keep a prayer journal as a way to develop and enrich her prayer life. Sometimes, the process of writing thoughts down leads to new insights and clarity (see **Write Your Prayer**).

The prayer journal itself can be a plain old notebook, a blank bound journal, or even a private blog.

Teens can use their prayer journal to write out their prayers, almost as if they were writing a letter to God. They can use their journal as an aid to meditation during **Lectio Divina** and the **Daily Examen**.

Alternatively, they can use the prayer journal as a place to reflect on their prayer experience—a habit encouraged by St. Ignatius of Loyola in his *Spiritual Exercises*. Some questions teens might want to consider when reflecting on their prayer experience:

- What was the mood or tone of my prayer—happy, sad, melancholy? (Ignatius emphasizes paying attention to emotions for clues about how we need to grow in the spiritual life.)

- What words or phrases or images were a theme in my prayer?

- What is God saying to me in my prayer?

Prayer Pillowcase

You can help kids learn simple morning or evening prayers by writing the prayers on their pillowcases using permanent marker or fabric marker. Put a morning prayer on one side and an evening prayer on the other; let the kids decorate the prayer with a border of flowers, stars and planets, etc. For detailed instructions, see this article at pbgrace.com.

You can also purchase Catholic prayer pillowcases with beautiful pictures of saints, angels, the Virgin Mary, and so on at PrayerPillowcases.com.

Prayer Placemats

Using large sheets of paper and (optionally) a laminating kit, make placemats featuring mealtime prayers or prayers for special liturgical feasts and seasons, and decorate them appropriately. Placemats celebrating the Feast of St. Francis (October 4), for example, might feature the St. Francis Prayer and be decorated with drawings of animals or scenes from nature.

Search for religious coloring pages online for younger children to use as part of their prayer placemats.

Prayer Prompts

One way to remind family members to pray is to post prayers, Scripture verses, and pious invocations (prayers as short as a phrase or sentence) in key places around your home. You can make your prayer prompts as simple as a handwritten Post-It note or as fancy as a professionally designed refrigerator magnet or plaque. For ideas, see **Bite-sized Biblical Prayer** and **Invocations**.

Here are some possible locations to post your prayer prompts:

- on the refrigerator door;

- on door frames leading out of bedrooms or out of the house;

- by the bathroom mirror (or on the bathroom mirror, using dry erase marker or soap);

- on the bathroom wall near the toilet;

- on a card dropped in a backpack or lunchbox;

- on the dashboard of your car;

- on the back of cereal boxes;

- on bedframes;

- at the table, using **Prayer Placemats** or **Table Triangles**.

Prayer Rugs

Use carpet squares as prayer rugs—a special place for younger children to sit during **Family Prayer Time**. Together with other environmental cues, a prayer rug can help children transition from ordinary play and family time to a special time with God. (See **Smells and Bells** for other ways to create a prayerful environment.)

Table Triangles

Table triangles are those triangular paper placards that many restaurants and fast food chains leave on their tables to advertise their specials. You can make a Table Triangle of your own by folding a piece of paper or cardstock into thirds and printing a different mealtime prayer on each side. Let one family member choose a mealtime prayer from the "menu" presented on the table triangle.

Wear Your Prayer

Older children and teens may be interested in wearing an outward sign of their faith—a reminder that they belong to God, and an encouragement to live out that reality in their everyday lives.

Besides the obvious religious-themed jewelry (cross necklaces, bracelets, etc.) and t-shirts, there are a number of other options for kids to "wear" their prayer, some of them uniquely Catholic:

Prayer wristband. You can purchase silicone wristbands with short prayers or statements of faith on them, or make your own custom wristbands online.

Rosary ring or bracelet. As the name implies, these rings and bracelets include beads to help the wearer pray the rosary anywhere. (A traditional set of rosary beads should not be worn as a necklace.)

Chastity ring. A chastity ring—also known as a purity ring or promise ring—is worn on the left hand's ring finger to symbolize the wearer's commitment to remain chaste until marriage.

Medals. Catholics have traditionally worn various medals as an outward sign of their inner devotion to Jesus. The most famous of these is the Miraculous Medal that the Virgin Mary gave to St. Catherine Laboure during a vision; others include the St. Michael and St. Christopher medals.

Scapular. A devotional scapular is a type of sacramental that usually consists of two small, rectangular pieces of cloth connected by longer strips of cloth. Often, the rectangular pieces of cloth contain devotional text or images. The scapular is worn over the shoulders, usually underneath clothing, with one piece of cloth against the wearer's chest and one on the wearer's back. Tradition holds that the Virgin Mary gave the devotional scapular to St. Simon Stock in the thirteenth century. The scapular is not only an outward sign of the wearer's devotion to Jesus and Mary, but as a sacramental, helps the wearer be more open to God's grace.

A Final Word: Pray for Your Children
As parents, we have the power (and responsibility) to introduce our children to God, and to the many ways of prayer that bring us closer to him. In the end, though, we cannot *control* our children's relationship with God. By its very nature, it must be each child's own freely given response to God's invitation.

What we can do, however, besides being intentional about nurturing our kids' faith, is to pray for them.

We can pray for them when they are sleeping. We can pray for them when they are away at school. We can pray for them, most especially, in that moment just before we discipline them.

We can pray that they will be safe, and that they will grow into the persons they were made to be.

We can pray that when the world hurts them, as it surely will, they might take their pain to Jesus crucified, so that, through the power of his Resurrection, he might transform that pain into something good.

We can pray that their hearts will become ever more generous and open to others, so that they might grow in their capacity to receive God's love.

We can pray that they will know true love, and have the courage to truly love.

And we can pray, above all, that they will one day know God face to face, and so enter into an abundance of joy and happiness, pressed down and overflowing.

A Handful of Catholic Prayers

Essential Catholic Prayers

Sign of the Cross

In the name of the Father,
and of the Son,
and of the Holy Spirit.
Amen.

*Touch your forehead on the word **Father**,*
*touch your chest on the word **Son**,*
*touch your left shoulder on the word **Holy**,*
*touch your right shoulder on the word **Spirit**,*
*and fold your hands on the word **Amen**.*

Use the Sign of the Cross to open and close your time of prayer.

Our Father

Our Father who art in heaven,
hallowed be thy name.
Thy kingdom come,
thy will be done
on earth as it is in heaven.
Give us this day our daily bread,
and forgive us our trespasses,
as we forgive those who trespass against us,
and lead us not into temptation,
but deliver us from evil.
Amen.

Hail Mary

Hail, Mary, full of grace,
the Lord is with thee;
blessed art thou among women,
and blessed is the fruit of thy womb, Jesus.
Holy Mary, Mother of God,
pray for us sinners,
now and at the hour of our death.
Amen.

Glory Be

Glory to the Father, and to the Son, and to the Holy Spirit: as
it was in the beginning, is now, and will be forever.
Amen.

The Apostles' Creed

I believe in God,
the Father almighty,
Creator of heaven and earth,
and in Jesus Christ, his only Son, our Lord,
who was conceived by the Holy Spirit,
born of the Virgin Mary,
suffered under Pontius Pilate,
was crucified, died and was buried;
he descended into hell;
on the third day he rose again from the dead;
he ascended into heaven,
and is seated at the right hand of God the Father almighty;
from there he will come to judge the living and the dead.
I believe in the Holy Spirit,
the holy catholic Church,
the communion of saints,
the forgiveness of sins,
the Resurrection of the body,
and life everlasting.
Amen.

Lasallian Call to Prayer

Let us remember that we are in the holy presence of God.

Morning Offerings

Morning Offering

O Jesus, through the Immaculate Heart of Mary,
I offer you my prayers, works, joys, and sufferings of this day
for all the intentions of your Sacred Heart,
in union with the Holy Sacrifice of the Mass
throughout the world,
for the salvation of souls, the reparation for sins,
the reunion of all Christians,
and in particular for the intentions of the
Holy Father this month.
Amen.

This Is the Day That the Lord Has Made (Psalm 118:24)

This is the day the Lord has made;
let us be glad and rejoice in it!

You can hear the sung version of this simple prayer at pbgrace.com.

A Short Morning Offering for Children

Thank you, God, for giving us this day;
help us to be like Jesus in all we think, do, and say.
Amen.

Angel of God

Angel of God, my guardian dear,
to whom God's love commits me here,
ever this day be at my side,
to light, to guard, to rule, and guide.
Amen.

Canticle of Zechariah (Benedictus)

Blessed be the Lord, the God of Israel;
he has come to His people and set them free.
He has raised up for us a mighty savior,
born of the house of His servant David.
Through his holy prophets he promised of old
that he would save us from our enemies,
from the hands of all who hate us.
He promised to show mercy to our fathers
and to remember his holy Covenant.
This was the oath he swore to our father Abraham:
to set us free from the hands of our enemies,
free to worship him without fear,
holy and righteous in his sight
all the days of our life.
You, my child, shall be called the prophet of the Most High;
for you will go before the Lord to prepare his way,
to give his people knowledge of salvation
by the forgiveness of their sins.
In the tender compassion of our God
the dawn from on high shall break upon us,
to shine on those who dwell in darkness
and the shadow of death,
and to guide our feet into the way of peace.

Glory to the Father, and to the Son, and to the Holy Spirit: as it was in the beginning, is now, and will be forever. Amen.

Noon Offerings

Angelus

Leader: The angel of the Lord declared unto Mary,
Response: And she conceived of the Holy Spirit.
Say the Hail Mary:
Hail, Mary, full of grace . . .
Leader: Behold the handmaid of the Lord.
Response: Be it done unto me according to thy Word.
Hail, Mary, full of grace . . .
Leader: And the Word was made flesh.
Response: And dwelt amongst us.
Hail, Mary, full of grace . . .
Leader: Pray for us, O Holy Mother of God.
Response: That we may be made worthy of the promises of Christ.
Leader: Let us pray: Pour forth, we beseech thee, O Lord, thy grace into our hearts, that we to whom the incarnation of Christ Thy Son was made known by the message of an angel, may by His Passion and cross be brought to the glory of His Resurrection; through the same Christ our Lord.
Response: Amen.

Regina Caeli

Leader: Queen of Heaven, rejoice, alleluia.
Response: For He whom you did merit to bear, alleluia.
Leader: Has risen, as he said, alleluia.
Response: Pray for us to God, alleluia.
Leader: Rejoice and be glad, O Virgin Mary, alleluia.
Response: For the Lord has truly risen, alleluia.
Leader: Let us pray. O God, who gave joy to the world through the Resurrection of Thy Son, our Lord Jesus Christ, grant we beseech Thee, that through the intercession of the Virgin Mary, His Mother, we may obtain the joys of everlasting life. Through the same Christ our Lord.
Amen.

Evening Offerings

Children's Bedside Prayer

Bless me, Lord, as this day ends,
Bless my family and all my friends,
Keep me safe throughout the night,
and wake me with the morning's light

Now I Lay Me Down to Sleep

Now I lay me down to sleep,
I pray the Lord my soul to keep.
Angels watch me through the night,
And wake me with the morning light.

Canticle of Mary (Magnificat)

My soul proclaims the greatness of the Lord,
my spirit rejoices in God my Savior
for he has looked with favor on his lowly servant.
From this day all generations will call me blessed:
the Almighty has done great things for me,
and holy is his Name.
He has mercy on those who fear him
in every generation.
He has shown the strength of his arm,
he has scattered the proud in their conceit.
He has cast down the mighty from their thrones,
and has lifted up the lowly.
He has filled the hungry with good things,
and the rich he has sent away empty.
He has come to the help of his servant Israel
for he has remembered his promise of mercy,
the promise he made to our fathers,
to Abraham and his children for ever.

Canticle of Simeon

Lord, now you let your servant go in peace;
your word has been fulfilled.
My eyes have seen the salvation
you have prepared in the sight of every people,
a light to reveal you to the nations and the glory of your
people, Israel.

An Evening Family Prayer (Robert Louis Stevenson)

Lord, behold our family here assembled.
We thank you for this place in which we dwell,
for the love that unites us,
for the peace accorded to us this day,
for the hope with which we expect the morrow;
for the health, the work, the food and the bright skies
that make our lives delightful;
for our friends in all parts of the earth.
Amen.

Phos Hilaron

O radiant light, O sun divine
of God the Father's deathless face,
O image of the light sublime
that fills the heav'nly dwelling place.
Lord Jesus Christ, as daylight fades,
as shine the lights of eventide,
we praise the Father with the Son,
the Spirit blest and with them one.
O Son of God, the source of life,
praise is your due by night and day;
unsullied lips must raise the strain
of your proclaimed and splendid name.

Mealtime Blessings

Bless us, O Lord

Bless us, O Lord,
and these your gifts
which we are about to receive
from your bounty,
through Christ, our Lord.
Amen.

Thank You, Jesus

Thank you, Jesus, for this food.
Amen.

Come, Lord Jesus

Come, Lord Jesus,
be our guest;
let these gifts
to us be blessed.
Amen.

Johnny Appleseed

This is a sung prayer; the melody is available at pbgrace.com.

O, the Lord is good to me!
And so I thank the Lord
for giving me
the things I need:
the sun, the rain, and the apple seed!
The Lord is good to me.
Amen! Amen! Amen, amen, amen!
Amen!

Prayers of the Saints

Prayer to St. Michael

St. Michael the Archangel,
defend us in battle;
be our protection against the wickedness and snares
of the devil.
May God rebuke him, we humbly pray:
and do thou, O Prince of the heavenly host,
by the power of God,
thrust into hell Satan and all the evil spirits
who prowl about the world seeking the ruin of souls.
Amen.

Prayer of St. Francis

Lord, make me an instrument of your peace;
where there is hatred, let me sow love;
where there is injury, pardon;
where there is error, truth;
where there is doubt, faith;
where there is despair, hope;
where there is darkness, light;
and where there is sadness, joy.
O Divine Master, grant that I may not so much seek
to be consoled as to console;
to be understood as to understand;
to be loved as to love.
For it is in giving that we receive;
it is in pardoning that we are pardoned;
and it is in dying that we are born to eternal life.

Canticle of the Sun (St. Francis)

Most high, all powerful, all good Lord!
All praise is Yours, all glory, all honor, and all blessing.
To You, alone, Most High, do they belong.
No mortal lips are worthy to pronounce Your name.
Be praised, my Lord, through all Your creatures,
especially through my lord Brother Sun,
who brings the day; and You give light through him.
And he is beautiful and radiant in all his splendor!
Of You, Most High, he bears the likeness.
Be praised, my Lord, through Sister Moon and the stars;
in the heavens You have made them bright, precious and
beautiful.
Be praised, my Lord, through Brothers Wind and Air,

and clouds and storms, and all the weather,
through which You give Your creatures sustenance.
Be praised, my Lord, through Sister Water;
she is very useful, and humble, and precious, and pure.
Be praised, my Lord, through Brother Fire,
through whom You brighten the night.
He is beautiful and cheerful, and powerful and strong.
Be praised, my Lord, through our sister Mother Earth,
who feeds us and rules us,
and produces various fruits with colored flowers and herbs.
Be praised, my Lord, through those who forgive for love of
You;
through those who endure sickness and trial.
Happy those who endure in peace,
for by You, Most High, they will be crowned.
Be praised, my Lord, through our sister Bodily Death,
from whose embrace no living person can escape.
Woe to those who die in mortal sin!
Happy those she finds doing Your most holy will.
The second death can do no harm to them.
Praise and bless my Lord, and give thanks,
and serve Him with great humility.

The Rosary

How to Say the Rosary

You don't need an actual string of rosary beads to pray the
Rosary, but it is traditional; the beads add a tactile dimension
to the prayer that reflects the sacramental, incarnational sensi-
bility of Catholic faith.

The prayers listed in bold can be found under **Essential Catholic Prayers** above.

1. Holding the crucifix, make the **Sign of the Cross**.

2. Then say the **Apostles' Creed**.

3. On the first large bead above the crucifix, say an **Our Father**.

4. On each of the next three smaller beads, pray a **Hail Mary**. (Traditionally, these are prayed for the intention of an increase of faith, an increase of hope, and an increase of charity.)

5. Then pray the **Glory Be**.

The main part of the rosary is divided up into five "decades," or sets of ten small beads. A different mystery of the rosary is contemplated during each decade. A decade of the rosary is prayed as follows:

6. Announce the mystery of the rosary to be contemplated, e.g., "The Agony in the Garden," along with any special intentions (e.g., for a sick relative, or for an end to war, etc.).

7. On the first large bead before the decade, pray the **Our Father.**

8. Say the **Hail Mary** on each of the ten small beads that make up the decade.

9. At the end of the decade, pray the **Glory Be**.

10. Some Catholics will add optional prayers at the end of each decade, such as the Fatima Prayer, the Miraculous Medal Prayer, or the O Sacrament Most Holy Prayer.

11. Repeat steps 6 through 10 for each of the remaining decades of the rosary.

12. After completing the fifth decade, many Catholics pray the **Hail, Holy Queen** (below), the **Canticle of Mary** (above), or other additional prayers.

13. Conclude with the **Sign of the Cross**.

Usually, when the rosary is prayed in a group setting, one person leads by saying the first half of the Apostles' Creed and each Our Father, Hail Mary, and Glory Be, while the entire group says the second half of each prayer.

See **Pray the Rosary** for ways to modify the rosary for use with children.

Mysteries of the Rosary
When talking about the "mysteries" of the rosary with kids, it might be helpful to explain that the word is meant not in the sense of a riddle to be solved, but in the sense of the divine, which is normally beyond human comprehension, being revealed in the life of Christ.

Here are the mysteries of the rosary:

The Joyful Mysteries
1. The Annunciation
The angel Gabriel announces to Mary that she is to be the mother of Jesus.

2. The Visitation
Mary visits her cousin Elizabeth, who is pregnant with John

the Baptist, and the two women praise God for his saving
work.

3. The Nativity
*Through the birth of Jesus, God comes to meet humanity "in
the flesh."*

4. The Presentation
*Mary and Joseph fulfill the Jewish law by presenting Jesus to
God in the Temple.*

5. The Finding of Jesus in the Temple
*After searching for the child Jesus for three days, Mary and
Joseph find him among the teachers in the Temple.*

The Luminous Mysteries
1. The Baptism of Jesus in the River Jordan
*John baptizes Jesus, and God proclaims that Jesus is his
beloved Son.*

2. The Wedding Feast at Cana
*In a prefiguring of the Eucharist, Jesus turns water into wine
at the request of his mother.*

3. The Proclamation of the Kingdom of God
*Through his preaching, Jesus calls people to conversion so
that God might reign in their lives.*

4. The Transfiguration of Jesus
*Jesus goes with Peter, James, and John to a mountaintop,
where his glory is revealed.*

5. The Institution of the Eucharist
Jesus offers his body and blood for the salvation of the world at the Last Supper.

The Sorrowful Mysteries
1. The Agony in the Garden
Jesus prays in the garden of Gethsemane on the night of his arrest.

2. The Scourging at the Pillar
Pontius Pilate has Jesus whipped while tied to a pillar.

3. The Crowning With Thorns
Roman soldiers mock Jesus as "king of the Jews" by crowning him with thorns.

4. The Carrying of the Cross
Jesus carries the cross to the place of his crucifixion.

5. The Crucifixion
Jesus is nailed to the cross and dies.

The Glorious Mysteries
1. The Resurrection
Jesus rises from the dead.

2. The Ascension
Jesus returns to his Father in heaven.

3. The Descent of the Holy Spirit at Pentecost
The Holy Spirit descends on the disciples, gathered in the upper room with Mary, and the Church is born.

4. The Assumption of Mary
Mary is assumed into heaven, body and soul.

5. The Coronation of Mary
Mary is crowned as queen of Heaven and Earth.

Hail, Holy Queen (Salve Regina)

Hail, holy Queen, Mother of Mercy,
hail our life, our sweetness and our hope.
To thee do we cry, poor banished children of Eve;
to thee do we send up our sighs,
mourning and weeping in this valley of tears.
Turn then, most gracious advocate,
thine eyes of mercy toward us;
and after this our exile,
show unto us the blessed fruit of thy womb, Jesus.
O clement, O loving, O sweet Virgin Mary.
Leader: Pray for us O holy Mother of God. . .
Response: . . . that we may be made worthy of the promises
of Christ.

Other Handy Prayers to Know

An Examination of Conscience for Children

The following examination of conscience is by Fr. Thomas Weinandy.

Responsibilities to God:

- Have I prayed every day?

- Have I prayed my morning prayers and night prayers?

- Have I prayed with my parents and family?

- Have I been moody and rebellious about praying and going to church on Sunday?

- Have I asked the Holy Spirit to help me whenever I have been tempted to sin?

- Have I asked the Holy Spirit to help me do what is right?

Responsibilities to others:

- Have I been obedient and respectful to my parents?

- Have I lied or been deceitful to them or to others?

- Have I been arrogant, stubborn or rebellious?

- Have I talked back to parents, teachers or other adults?

- Have I pouted and been moody?

- Have I been selfish toward my parents, brothers, and sisters, teachers, or my friends and schoolmates?

- Have I gotten angry at them? Have I hit anyone?

- Have I held grudges or not forgiven others?

- Have I treated other children with respect or have I made fun of them and called them names?

- Have I used bad language?

- Have I stolen anything? Have I returned it?

- Have I performed my responsibilities, such as homework and household chores?

- Have I been helpful and affectionate toward my family?

- Have I been kind and generous with my friends?

Pope Francis' Five-Finger Prayer

This simple aid to prayer has been popularized by Pope Francis, and it's perfect for kids.

14. The thumb is the closest finger to you. So start praying for those who are closest to you. They are the persons easiest to remember. To pray for our dear ones is a "sweet obligation."

15. The next finger is the index finger. Pray for those who teach you, instruct you, and heal you. They need God's help as they offer direction for others.

16. The following finger is the tallest. It reminds us of our government leaders and others who have authority. They need God's guidance.

17. The fourth finger is the ring finger, which is also our weakest finger. It should remind us to pray for the weakest

among us—the sick, the poor, those excluded from society, and those plagued by other problems.

18. And finally we have our smallest finger, the smallest of all. Your pinkie should remind you to pray for yourself. When you are done praying for the other four groups, you will be able to pray for your own needs in a better way.

Eternal Rest

This prayer is often said upon learning of the death of a friend or relative.

Eternal rest grant unto them, O Lord, and let perpetual light shine upon them. May the souls of the faithful departed, through the mercy of God, rest in peace. Amen.

Memorare

Remember, O most gracious Virgin Mary, that never was it known that anyone who fled to thy protection, implored thy help, or sought thine intercession was left unaided.

Inspired by this confidence, I fly unto thee, O Virgin of virgins, my mother; to thee do I come, before thee I stand, sinful and sorrowful. O Mother of the Word Incarnate, despise not my petitions, but in thy mercy hear and answer me.
Amen.

Anima Christi

Soul of Christ, sanctify me;
Body of Christ, save me;
Blood of Christ, inebriate me;
Water from Christ's side, wash me;
Passion of Christ, strengthen me.
O good Jesus, hear me;
within Thy wounds hide me.
Suffer me not to be separated from Thee;
from the malicious enemy defend me;
in the hour of my death call me,
and bid me come unto Thee
that I may praise Thee with Thy saints
and with Thy angels
Forever and ever.
Amen.

A Quick-Find Index of Prayer Ideas and Handy Checklist

Following is an index of most of the ideas and suggestions in this book; it also doubles as a checklist. Check off every idea you have tried as a family, not with the goal of completing the whole list, but of trying a wide variety of prayer styles.

☐ Bonus points for participation
☐ Check out Scriptural connections
☐ Consequences
☐ Do a liturgical scavenger hunt
☐ Educate your kids about the Eucharistic liturgy
☐ Encourage service in appropriate liturgical ministries
☐ Explain what is going on
☐ Give kids a missal
☐ Give kids a prayer book
☐ Give young children a Holy Card Key Chain
☐ Introduce your child to the priest, lectors, musicians, and servers
☐ Invite participation
☐ Make a point to offer thanks
☐ Play Mass at home
☐ Pray for help, and don't expect perfection
☐ Provide a missal
☐ Read and discuss the Scripture readings in advance
☐ Sit up front
☐ Unpack the Mass
☐ Use the nursery or cry room
☐ Walk through the Mass
☐ Walk to Mass

☐ **Celebrate Reconciliation 59**
   ☐ Coach reconciliation
   ☐ Develop a habit
   ☐ Find a time that works
   ☐ Go early
   ☐ Help kids overcome nervousness
   ☐ Identify obstacles
   ☐ Model reconciliation
   ☐ Practice a Daily Examen

- [ ] **Morning Prayer 31**
- [ ] **Noon Prayer 32**
- [ ] Pray the Scriptures with Little Helpers
- [ ] Sing your Prayer
- [ ] Teach classic mealtime prayers
- [ ] **Novenas 95**
- [ ] **Paper Chain Prayers 133**
- [ ] **Pray Before School 33**
- [ ] At the door
- [ ] At the flagpole
- [ ] In the car
- [ ] **Pray Comings and Goings 34**
- [ ] **Pray for the Dead 97**
- [ ] Keep a calendar of death anniversaries
- [ ] Mark death anniversaries with prayer and ritual
- [ ] **Pray for Emergency Vehicles 34**
- [ ] **Pray the Five Forms of Prayer 98**
- [ ] blessing and adoration
- [ ] intercession
- [ ] petition praise
- [ ] thanksgiving
- [ ] **Pray Life Events 35**
  - [ ] addiction
  - [ ] adoption
  - [ ] baptismal anniversary
  - [ ] beginning or ending a school year
  - [ ] birthdays
  - [ ] blessing objects (such as tools, art materials, home, family vehicle, products of nature)
  - [ ] childbirth
  - [ ] discernment
  - [ ] engagement to be married

- [ ] financial difficulties
- [ ] graduation
- [ ] harvesting
- [ ] leaving home (for an extended period of time)
- [ ] miscarriage
- [ ] moving
- [ ] neighborhood or family strife
- [ ] nursing or feeding a child
- [ ] planting
- [ ] retirement
- [ ] sports events
- [ ] study
- [ ] travel
- [ ] unemployment
- [ ] weather
- [ ] wedding anniversary
- [ ] welcoming guests
- [ ] work
- [ ] **Pray the Our Father Meditatively 100**
  - [ ] Pray it with the *Catechism*
  - [ ] Use books and videos
  - [ ] Paraphrase the meaning for kids
- [ ] **Pray the Rosary 101**
  - [ ] Ignore the kids and pray
  - [ ] Look for cool supplemental resources
  - [ ] Make your own cord rosaries
  - [ ] Pray the Scriptural rosary
  - [ ] Set a prayerful mood
  - [ ] Shorten the decades
  - [ ] Skip the beads, or get kid- friendly ones
  - [ ] Start with one decade
  - [ ] Use pictures to aid meditation

Acknowledgments

Special thanks to members of Parenting with the Spirit for their ideas and suggestions, particularly during the initial brainstorming process: Annie Casselman; Amy Donnenwerth; Kate Errthum; Shana Johnson; Renee Knutson; Carrie McKee; Sara Moore; Andrea Teska; Marcy Van Fossen; and Robyn Wangberg. Members of the Peanut Butter and Grace Facebook discussion group also shared their ideas, insights, and experiences. The group is private, so I won't mention them by name; they know who they are.

I am indebted to the wisdom gleaned from the many wise and wonderful moms and dads I met through Early Childhood Family Education classes over the years. During my time at ECFE, I developed a deep respect for the ability of the staff to dispense practical wisdom in a nonthreatening way—and to just listen, when that is what a distressed parent needs most. They "minister" God's grace with compassion and humor every day. In particular, Katy Smith, Jennifer McHugh, and Chris Overhaug have not only been wise mentors, but good friends as well.

Special thanks to parenting "expert" and mentor Annmarie DeMarais for reviewing an early draft of this book, and offering suggestions to improve its organization. Barbara and Jim Allaire offered their suggestions and encouragement, and have been mentors to me in my faith development.

My parents, Pat and Norman Daoust, sat us kids down for "family time" (catechesis) once a week and "prayer time" every night; their overall approach planted the seeds that became this book. They are representative of generations of parents who quietly and faithfully practiced family-based faith formation before it had a fancy name or an instruction manual.

Finally, thanks to my wife, Susan, and my children (Benjamin, Maria, Julia, Matthew, and Alex). They have patiently put up with my many experiments in family prayer and catechesis over the years . . . some of which worked better than others. Thanks for teaching me many things along the way, with love and laughter; you have been my school for living in the Kingdom of God.